Military Reengineering Between the World Wars

Brett Steele

T0159310

Prepared for the Office of the Secretary of Defense

Approved for public release; distribution unlimited

NATIONAL DEFENSE RESEARCH INSTITUTE

The research described in this report was prepared for the Office of the Secretary of Defense (OSD). The research was conducted in the RAND National Defense Research Institute, a federally funded research and development center supported by the OSD, the Joint Staff, the unified commands, and the defense agencies under Contract DASW01-01-C-0004.

Library of Congress Cataloging-in-Publication Data

Steele, Brett D.
    Military reengineering between the World Wars / Brett Steele.
        p. cm.
    "MG-253."
    Includes bibliographical references.
    ISBN 0-8330-3721-8 (pbk. : alk. paper)
        1. Armed Forces—Reorganization—History—20th century. 2. Armed Forces—
    Technological innovations. 3. Internal combustion engines. 4. Motorization, Military—
    History. 5. Mechanization, Military—History. 6. Reengineering (Management) I.
    Title.

UA10.S65 2005
355.3'09'042—dc22

                                                                2005002945

The RAND Corporation is a nonprofit research organization providing objective analysis and effective solutions that address the challenges facing the public and private sectors around the world. RAND's publications do not necessarily reflect the opinions of its research clients and sponsors.

RAND® is a registered trademark.

Published 2005 by the RAND Corporation
1776 Main Street, P.O. Box 2138, Santa Monica, CA 90407-2138
1200 South Hayes Street, Arlington, VA 22202-5050
201 North Craig Street, Suite 202, Pittsburgh, PA 15213-1516
RAND URL: http://www.rand.org/
To order RAND documents or to obtain additional information, contact
Distribution Services: Telephone: (310) 451-7002;
Fax: (310) 451-6915; Email: order@rand.org

Preface

This monograph report initially served as a background study for a project assigned by the Commander, U.S. Joint Forces Command, and his Director of Joint Experimentation (J-9). It now incorporates additional research derived from a special crosscutting project for the Office of the Secretary of Defense (OSD) and the Joint Chiefs of Staff.

This research was conducted within the International Security Defense Research Center of the RAND Corporation's National Defense Research Institute, a federally funded research and development center (FFRDC) sponsored by OSD, the Joint Staff, the unified commands, and the defense agencies.

Comments are welcome and should be addressed to the project leader, Dr. Paul K. Davis, by e-mail at pdavis@rand.org.

For more information on RAND's International Security Policy Center, contact the director, James Dobbins. He can be reached by e-mail at James_Dobbins@rand.org; by phone at 703-413-1100, extension 5134; or by mail at the RAND Corporation, 1200 South Hayes Street, Arlington, VA, 22202-5050.

Contents

Foreword

By Stephen J. Cimbala

The subject of military transformation has by now filled bookshelves, and soon will fully occupy entire libraries. There are many valid perspectives that can be taken on transformation. The present study takes an original look at one kind of transformation: reengineering. Reengineering offers a unique point of departure for the understanding of military transformation. It is best to think of reengineering as a process of designed change in the way that organizations work. Reengineering, as applied to military organizations, comprehends the short- and mid-term adjustments that must be made in coadjusting new technology to (1) the design of future force structure, (2) the process of military decision making, and (3) the practice of military art at the operational and tactical levels.

Brett Steele's original and informative analysis of reengineering examines the efforts of militaries between the world wars of the 20th century to adapt to motorized and mechanized warfare made possible by the internal combustion engine. Some military forces were more successful than others: they were able to adapt their organizational processes to incorporate new ways of thinking about war and military art. Others failed to do so, at least in a timely manner and in as thorough a fashion as did their competition. Slow and incoherent reformers fell behind fast and organized innovators in the 1920s and 1930s, with results that played themselves out in World War II.

As Dr. Steele's study explains, success in reengineering was not a guarantee of victory in battle. Mastery of reengineering could only add to the probability of military effectiveness, other things being equal. Much else goes into determining the margin between victory and defeat. The interwar years witnessed some remarkable adaptations on the part of military planners and political leaders with respect to their expectations about future war. Other leaders and planners failed to fit new technology into a new paradigm for war. Human nature, organizational inertia, and vested interests in the status quo all played a part in derailing some reengineering into false starts.

The strong points of this monograph are many, but several stand out.

First, the term *reengineering* appeals to me as more specific and more suited to the subject matter than the currently fashionable *transformation*. The only concern is that, in some hands, reengineering might have a narrow military-technical focus. But that is not the case here.

Second, the author's conceptual model for the assessment of reengineering is original and sound. The summary section on the general features of successful reengineering is well explained and offers an important new perspective on this complex issue.

Third, the author's selection and treatment of historical cases are, in my judgment, very thoughtful and sustainable. I especially liked the case study of the Soviet army between the world wars. No 20th-century military force had to learn more, at a faster speed. The author's obvious enthusiasm about Tukhachevsky seduced me—my favorite Red Commander, a gifted scholar with the soul of a poet and fanatic revolutionary, meeting a fate only Russian history could provide.

Tukhachevsky's theory of deep battle is not only a historical footnote, but also a prelude to the Soviet Union's later Cold War "military-technical revolution" that preceded the United States' own "revolution in military affairs." This history, of Soviet innovative thinking in the 1920s and 1930s, also anticipates much of the vertical revolution in warfare with the earliest true airborne exercises. Thus the Soviet military thinking of the interwar years, although not necessarily the greater part of their organization and training, is a case study in anticipating the "army after next" beyond the generation of reform that is immediately over the horizon.

The case study of the Marine Corps is also well positioned. The performance of the Marines in the battle of Guadalcanal shows Yankee ingenuity at its best, along with the tenacity and esprit that makes the Marines unique. The truth is that the strategic planning that preceded

Guadalcanal was flawed, the decision to put it in motion was hurried, and the commitment of superordinate Navy commanders was halfhearted (Fletcher steamed away and left the Marines to their own devices, and Ghormley had to be relieved by Halsey). The necessary equipment for opposed landings that was later taken for granted in amphibious operations of this type was not available. Despite all these blunders by their civilian and military leaders, the Marines adapted, improvised, and overcame in their time-honored fashion.

However, the story of the Marines' adaptive learning about amphibious warfare is also a story of U.S. Navy resistance and military obfuscation. One might draw parallels between naval ambivalence about support for opposed landings and naval ambivalence with regard to carrier air warfare, or convoys. In each case the author has a strong point for the argument that reengineering is about new thinking, organization, and planning ("process") as much as it is about technological innovation per se. The British, French, and German cases, with regard to their treatment of armored warfare, make this point well.

Although the paper does allude to the importance of doctrine, additional emphasis might be placed on doctrine as a key element in the process of reengineering. Doctrine is the glue that holds together the strategic war-fighting concepts and operational-tactical styles of combatant forces. In the Red Army, the development of agreed doctrine was a matter of considerable controversy in the interwar years: careers were ruined or made, and manuals torn apart. But the result of doctrinal turbulence was military innovation that helped to prepare the Soviets for World War II.

Doctrine is significant, as well, because it captures not only the strategic concepts and operational-tactical proclivities of armies. It also expresses their soul-forces, or self-concepts of warriordom. This element cannot be factored apart from innovation, transformation, reengineering, or whatever you prefer to call it. The self-concept of a fighting force is what gets it to the finish line against long odds. The idea that "we" are special compared to "they" is not only a useful fiction but, in the hands of capable officers, it can be turned into an effective, empowering empirical fact. Think of the SS *Totenkopf,* the 62nd Guards Army, and the U.S. 101st and 82nd Airborne.

This important aspect of military doctrine also links forces to the society that supports them by defining a relationship between citizen and armed force. In the 1920s the Soviet armed-forces leadership was roiled by controversy over the form and content of a truly "Soviet" armed force. Some favored an army of a new type: revolutionary indoctrination and a mass of conscripts led by politically correct Red Commanders. Others argued that, whatever its link to society, the Red Army would have to meet modern standards of industrial development and corporate professional leadership.

I think the failures of the British, American, and French armies between the world wars are embedded in their confusions about self-concept. Armies that cannot answer the question "What am I?" with consensus and certainty are bound to have difficulty adjusting to new conditions in technology or, for that matter, in geopolitics. The French army is an interesting case of self-concept in search of permanent moorings. From the *élan vital* and offensive *a l'outrance* of World War I, it reversed itself and planned for a *bataille conduite* (methodical battle) in the 1920s and 1930s. This choice was less frivolous than it has appeared to many historians, and the author is right to credit the Maginot Line as having incorporated important innovations in fortified defense. What the French missed was a change in Germany's concept of fighting that would be based on the disruption of the enemy's cohesion by fast-moving panzer divisions and tactical air power. But even this revolutionary concept of military operations would not have been possible without the rebirth of the self-concept of invincible German arms, based on rebuilding of force structure, innovative technology, and, as important, doctrinal emphasis on combined arms training and fighting.

As a final note: the author's case studies show the pivotal role played by maverick individuals among technologists and strategists, against the grain of tradition and bureaucracy. Innovators must walk a fine line between constructive criticism and self-destructive irrelevancy. Why do some succeed and others fail? Turbulent times can throw up a Cromwell or a Napoléon, but few have the opportunity to remake entire states or armies in good time. Many reformers, especially in militaries, are pushed to the side and ignored until drastic conditions on the world stage force rethinking of strategy and military art.

In brief, for most mavericks to succeed, they require propitious environmental conditions (e.g., crisis or war) and help from the top. Most successful military innovators must master the art of bureaucracy even as they attempt to circumvent its most antireformist tendencies. One must maintain the appearance of a "team player" who does not seem to threaten the ethos of the organization as a whole. Neither British nor French army reformers were as successful as their German counterparts in the 1930s in this regard. In the Soviet Union, Tukhachevsky led the charge for reform until his brilliance so obviously overshadowed that of Stalin and his poodle proletarians that Tukhachevsky became an unacceptable political liability. This reminds us of More's law (as in St. Thomas More), equally as important as Moore's Law about innovation in microchips: the price for success in military or other organizational reform is often one's head. Most organizations are run by jealous mediocrities, or worse.

Summary

Introduction

Incorporating new technological innovations into military organizations has always subjected senior leadership to high degrees of risk, as exemplified by the advent of gunpowder, the steam engine, the telegraph, the radio, or the nuclear bomb.[1] The question is whether comparative historical study can illuminate successful strategies to mitigate such risk as well as caution against problematic approaches. This is a relevant policy question given the perceived military opportunities currently suggested

---

[1] For an in-depth discussion of gunpowder, see Bert S. Hall, *Weapons and Warfare in Renaissance Europe: Gunpowder, Technology, and Tactics*, Baltimore and London: Johns Hopkins University Press, 1997; and Geoffrey Parker, *The Military Revolution: Military Innovation and the Rise of the West, 1500–1800*, Cambridge: Cambridge University Press, 1988. On the subject of steam, see Dennis E. Showalter, *Railroads and Rifles: Soldiers, Technology, and the Unification of Germany*, Hamden, Conn.: Archon, 1975. For nuclear power, refer to such classic studies as A. J. Bacevich, *The Pentomic Era: The U.S. Army Between Korea and Vietnam*, Washington, D.C.: National Defense University Press, 1986; and Harvey M. Sapolsky, *The Polaris System Development: Bureaucratic and Programmatic Success in Government*, Cambridge, Mass.: Harvard University Press, 1972. For more generalized studies associated with the Revolution in Military Affairs campaign, see Andrew Krepenevich, "Cavalry to Computer: The Pattern of Military Revolution," *National Interest*, fall 1994, pp. 30–42; and Richard O. Hundley, *Past Revolutions, Future Transformations: What Can the History of Revolutions in Military Affairs Tell Us About Transforming the U.S. Military?* Santa Monica, Calif.: RAND Corporation, 1999; as well as the numerous other studies done for, or influenced by, Mr. Andrew Marshall, OSD's Director of Net Assessment. Some of these studies, including the work of Michael Vickers, have apparently not been formally published.

While this essay is not directly confronting the notion of "revolutionary" military change, it is implicitly arguing that *reengineering* may be a less problematic term, given the warnings that institutional economists have made about the dangers of seeking revolutionary change in complex organizations. See Douglas C. North, *Institutions, Institutional Change, and Economic Performance*, Cambridge: Cambridge University Press, 1990.

by the rapid growth of computer networks and processing power. Yet while fundamental combat strategies of attrition, annihilation, and counterinsurgency have persisted despite the particular technology involved, fundamental approaches to risky technological incorporation also exist.[2] To address these approaches, this work analyzes the contrasting military responses to the internal combustion engine between World War I and World War II through the lens of reengineering.

Reengineering, as the term is used here, denotes a fundamental change in an organization's processes. Such change results from a reasonably "managed" effort that is made possible by two conditions: the technology required either exists or is within reach, and the goals are reasonably well perceived.[3] Military forces can change, and even transform, in widely contrasting ways. Reengineering has particular relevance because it typically relates to near- and mid-term planning. Some reengineering campaigns are highly planned (i.e., the solutions are worked out in advance), whereas others are accomplished through more iterative innovation, experimentation, and full-scale operational testing. In the latter case, there may be many studies and rigorous analyses, but solutions are more often "discovered" than deduced a priori. It is also possible to start reengineering an organization's processes with a prototype effort that is relatively insulated from the organization as a whole. Its diffusion throughout the organization is only permitted when local success is assured.

The purpose of this work is to assess the military strategies for incorporating the internal combustion engine during the interwar period. Adopting the familiar point that it is one thing to adopt new technology and quite another to change an organization's basic pro-

---

[2] For the classic analysis of strategies of attrition and annihilation, see Hans Delbruck's three-volume series *History of the Art of War,* Lincoln, Nebr.: University of Nebraska Press, 1990. For a more recent analysis of counterinsurgency strategies, see Max Boot, *The Savage Wars of Peace: Small Wars and the Rise of American Power,* New York: Basic Books, 2002. For a comparative discussion of technological innovation strategies, see Brett D. Steele, "An Economic Theory of Technological Products," *Technological Forecasting and Social Change,* Vol. 48, No. 3, March 1995, pp. 221–242.

[3] For further discussion and definition, see Paul K. Davis, *Planning Force Transformations: Learning from Both Successes and Failures,* Santa Monica, Calif.: RAND Corporation, unpublished, 2001.

cesses and overall structure, this survey considers the following three sets: (1) nations that adopted technology but did not change their processes; (2) nations that both adopted technology and changed their processes (i.e., reengineered) but got the vision wrong; and (3) nations that both reengineered in response to new technology and got the vision largely right. Each set of national experiences offers basic strategic insights into the benefits and risks of reengineering in response to new technological opportunities.

In the interwar years, few disputed the need for tanks and motorized transport. The controversy concerned whether such machinery could be assimilated within established doctrines and processes or whether more fundamental changes were needed. Those advocating deeper changes faced the immense challenge of proving that the new technology, coupled with uncertain new processes, offered vast improvements in system performance. All of this should sound familiar in light of current debates about military transformation in response to new technological realities.

Military change in the interwar era is a popular topic in institutional military history. Historians, including Williamson Murray, Allan Millet, David Johnson, MacGregor Knox, and Timothy Foy, have generated a substantial body of knowledge in this domain. This monograph seeks to synthesize some of that literature by focusing on institutional responses to new internal-combustion-engine technology. It will in turn cast such familiar developments as the German Blitzkrieg tactic and the Soviet Operational Art in a different light, relative to popular historical perceptions.

Militaries That Assimilated Technology but Did Not Reengineer

Three significant interwar armies willingly adopted the tank while leaving basic military processes intact: the Italian, the British, and the American. The Fascist Italian army proved to be the most conservative: it displayed little formal imagination in developing military processes beyond the massed infantry and artillery tactics of World

War I, in spite of Italian experiments with mechanized and motorized warfare in Ethiopia and Spain. Only temporarily, the British and American armies showed creativity in their experimental studies of new armored-warfare processes. Like their Italian counterparts, the British and American senior commanders largely rejected or misanalyzed the results of their experiments, especially any evidence suggesting the utility of an independent armored division. They were willing to acquire motor-powered vehicles for both transportation and combat, but they were ultimately only willing to use them to marginally improve existing infantry, cavalry, and logistical processes. Surprisingly, such persistence lasted well into World War II, especially in the British army. Nonetheless, the Allied victory clearly shows that weak reengineering efforts in peacetime can be counterbalanced by highly adaptable troops in the field, prodigious acquisition capabilities, and a powerful, if not stoic, political will.

Militaries That Reengineered but Got It Wrong

The second set of forces willingly constructed new military processes (and organizations) but based such work on fallacious strategic assumptions. These included the French army, virtually all of the naval forces, and the U.S. Army Air Corps. The French ultimately procured the most technically superior tanks in Western Europe and incorporated them into their new combat doctrine, Methodical Battle. Informed by French experience on the Western Front in World War I, the doctrine maximized firepower and minimized the exposure of France's largely conscripted interwar army. The doctrine, however, proved to be ineffectual against the German offensive that took France by surprise in the Ardennes.

Both the Axis and Allied navies willingly funded the development of the airplane, the submarine, the assault craft, and other internal-combustion innovations introduced during World War I. Such technologies, though, merely enhanced the traditional primacy of the battleship. Yet it was only after Pearl Harbor (and even later for the Japanese) that carrier task forces were recognized universally as the superior tactical formation.

The U.S. Army Air Corps displayed more enthusiasm towards adopting both revolutionary technology and processes. It acquired the powerful B-17 bomber and pioneered the process of daytime precision bombing. Yet daytime precision bombing without escort proved infeasible, and the task of furnishing escorts proved perplexing. The theory, however persuasive, had been highly misleading. Reengineering in the aircraft industry for the mass production of aircraft and bombers nonetheless proved highly successful and went far to compensate for the shortcomings of the precision-bombing process.

Militaries That Reengineered and Got It Right

Some militaries conducted successful reengineering programs that reflected astute strategic analyses. The Soviet Red Army, under Marshal Tukhachevsky's guidance, was willing to invest heavily in the development and manufacturing of tanks, as well as the organization of independent tank divisions to be used in accord with the Deep Operation doctrine. Not well appreciated, however, was Tukhachevsky's success in convincing Stalin to coordinate his first Five-Year Plan to meet the Red Army's logistical requirements for lengthy attritional warfare. This formed the structure that the Soviets used to crush the Wehrmacht in 1943 and 1944, in spite of the purges of 1937 and their consequential defeats in 1941 and 1942.

By contrast, the Germans got the concepts right only during the initial short campaigns of World War II, which were characterized by an optimized distribution of motor-powered resources, along with combined-arms actions, demoralizing encirclement tactics, and frontline initiative. Nevertheless, they could not restrict their enemies to those easily intimidated by such capabilities; they failed profoundly to prepare for the war they eventually fought and lost—a long, bloody war of attrition in which production and logistics reigned supreme.

Unlike the German Wehrmacht, the U.S. Marine Corps managed to get their reengineering right in the long run. Still saddled with its traditional reputation as secondary naval troops in spite of its valor in World War I, the Marine Corps quickly seized on the seemingly impossible process of amphibious assault against active fortified defenses. It adopted this strategy in light of the Allied experience in Gallipoli and its traditional coastal-fortification doctrines. This in turn reflected the Marines' need for a unique combat mission to ensure institutional survival and to prepare for the looming strategic realities of Japanese expansion into the central Pacific during World War I. It also reflected their faith in the development of suitable motor-powered assault vessels. The Marines' strategic vision and reengineering efforts were sound and central to the Pacific campaign, however stressful initial application proved to be at Guadalcanal and Tarawa.

Despite their relatively successful reengineering attempts, the Red Army, the Wehrmacht, and the U.S. Marine Corps all experienced serious shortfalls when their new forces were exposed to combat. Yet, because of effective feedback processes during World War II, they were able to iterate—building heavily upon, but correcting errors of, their peacetime reengineering efforts. For the Germans, however, such feedback came too late to avoid catastrophic defeat.

Lessons to Be Learned: Necessary Conditions?

Based on this comparative overview, five apparently necessary conditions for military reengineering emerge. The first is the willingness to exploit new technological opportunities systematically through research, education, training, and experimentation. The second is the ability to anticipate and prepare for the range of future strategic demands through historical awareness, strategic analysis, and the ability to transcend immediate political pressures in order to comprehend looming threats. The third condition involves securing sufficient resources (financial, material, and human) for the reengineering process—both externally from civilian political authorities and internally from the military ranks. The fourth is the ability to balance the two fundamental military cultures: the skilled yet traditional warrior and the scientific or rational analyst. The perspectives of both are essential for successful reengineering; failure is perhaps guaranteed when one faction dominates. The fifth and final condition is the ability to objectively diagnose weaknesses in the reengineered processes and to proceed to correct them expeditiously: getting things right from the start through reason and prior experience alone is difficult, if not impossible.

Running across these five conditions is the need to engage in open, objective debate and analysis, as well as to assess the results: strong leaders often get things wrong, even badly wrong. Another lesson is that large-scale reengineering usually follows years of smaller-scale efforts, because (1) it takes time to understand problems and develop solutions, even when technology is at hand and broad direction is understood, and (2) organizational resistance to change is very strong until necessity is manifested unambiguously or until a new generation of leaders takes over without the same vested interests.

Acknowledgments

This paper is a direct result of Paul Davis's guidance with both its conception and formulation. In addition to his valuable perspective, I also value the useful insights of colleagues David E. Johnson, Jefferson Marquis, RAND consultants Professor Paul Bracken of Yale University and Professor Stephen Cimbala of Penn State University. I am also grateful to Tamera Dorland for her much-needed perspectives. Any inaccuracies remain mine alone.

Abbreviations

FFRDC	federally funded research and development center
FLEX	fleet landing exercises
FMF	Fleet Marine Force
LCM	Landing Craft, Medium
LCT	Landing Craft, Tracked
LCVP	Landing Craft, Vehicle, Personnel, and Ramp
LVT	Landing Vehicles Tank
MCS	Marine Corps School
NACA	National Advisory Committee for Aeronautics
NCO	noncommissioned officer
NKVD	Russian People's Commissariat of Internal Affairs
OSD	Office of the Secretary of Defense
RAF	Royal Air Force
R&D	research and development

CHAPTER ONE

Introduction

Purpose

This paper was stimulated by the belief that a significant portion of the transformation currently sought for U.S. forces should be viewed as an exercise in reengineering in response to technological change.[1] It is therefore useful to review historical transformations that exemplify reengineering (although the word did not yet exist) to determine whether there are identifiable factors that make the difference between success and failure. The paper's purpose, then, is to survey a range of military developments during the period between World Wars I and II. Its focus is on efforts to exploit the internal combustion engine. Many of the cases discussed will be familiar to readers, but the reengineering perspective taken here appears to be original.

Approach

As Andrew Marshall has argued, there are many parallels between the interwar and post–Cold War eras.[2] Just as today's U.S. forces are trans-

---

[1] Paul K. Davis, *Planning Force Transformation: Learning from Both Successes and Failures*, Santa Monica, Calif.: RAND Corporation, unpublished, 2001.

[2] Andrew W. Marshall, "Some Thoughts on Military Revolutions," (Office of Net Assessment [OSD/NA] memorandum, Washington, D.C., July 27, 1993). p. 2. The similarity is even more apparent following the U.S. invasions of Afghanistan and Iraq, given their status as low-level counterinsurgency wars that distract from the preparation of high-tech wars against peer competitors. Of the major Western powers, only the Germans, ironically, were totally spared from the distraction of active "imperial duties," thanks to the Treaty of Versailles.

forming themselves to take advantage of civilian advances in computing technology, the interwar armies sought to optimize their capabilities through adopting the internal combustion engine. The forces in these two eras also suffered comparably from uncertainty as to (1) how best to use the new technology, (2) whether the necessary investments were justified by the likely enemies, and (3) what changes in military concepts and military organization would be needed to maximize the value of the technology. The two eras also included wildly fluctuating economic constraints, popular sentiments that full-scale warfare was irrational and obsolete, and assumptions that the military status quo was more than sufficient to handle all conceivable military contingencies. The parallels, then, are considerable.

A key element of military transformation is the design and incorporation of new *processes* to use the new technology effectively. By *process,* I am referring to flows of information, resources, and constraints—how people interact, coordinate, and solve problems within an organization. The design of new processes in a reasonably "managed" effort will be designated here as *reengineering*, especially when the proposed change is either unobvious or profound. The technical details of designing new internal combustion engines and their accompanying military vehicles in the 1920s and 1930s have little to offer today's military reformers. Nonetheless, the institutional challenges of reengineering are relatively universal. The resistance confronting the Ottoman sultans, who sought to incorporate firearms into their horse-archer armies during the mid-15th century, had remarkable parallels to the resistance facing generals who struggled to employ tanks in their foot-infantry armies during the early 20th century.[3] Both technologies proved to be highly threatening to the cultural identity of established military organizations.

In this paper, I treat developing and adopting new technology, and developing and adopting new military processes (along with re-

---

[3] The Ottomans ultimately chose the drastic reengineering option of creating an entirely new military organization, the Janissary Corps, to incorporate successfully the new technology of gunpowder during the 15th century. For a concise overview, see David Nicolle, *The Janissaries*, Oxford: Osprey Publishing, 1995.

lated changes of organization), as independent variables. As Andrew Marshall and others have discussed for some time, the most effective military organizations are those able and willing to do both.[4] In what follows, we shall look at interwar military organizations that were willing to incorporate new applications of the internal combustion engine but were unable to reengineer their basic military processes. These include the American, British, and Italian armies. Then we will examine those forces that were willing to incorporate both new applications of the internal combustion engine and new processes while failing to develop a robust concept of the future. These include the French army and the U.S. Army Air Corps, as well as the navies of Japan, Great Britain, Germany, Italy, and the United States. Then we will turn our attention to those organizations that incorporated the new internal-combustion technology, engaged in profound reengineering efforts, and correctly oriented their transformation to include preparations for the actual war that would be fought. These include the Soviet Red Army, the U.S. Marine Corps, and, to a lesser degree, the German Wehrmacht.

In some cases, successes were astonishing, although they were usually accompanied by errors. No one did everything right.

Such a historical analysis is applied in the last, analytical part of the paper, which identifies factors necessary for success. These include exploiting technological opportunities, anticipating strategic demands, securing sufficient political resources, managing military-cultural balances, and improving performance through evaluation and feedback.

The paper's goal is not to construct teleological or "presentist" lists of history's geniuses and idiots. Instead, it seeks to illustrate the challenges of military reengineering, efficiently and dramatically, in terms of both success and failure.

---

[4] More precisely, Marshall stated in "Some Thoughts on Military Revolutions" (1993) that a revolution in military affairs occurs when "the incorporation of new technology into military systems combines with innovative operational concepts and organizational adaptations to fundamentally alter the character and conduct of military operations."

Basic Definitions

To avoid unnecessary confusion, some clarifications are necessary. *Transformation* is used here to convey a fundamental shift in the relationship among the financial investment, operational cost, and technical performance that an organization can deliver. It entails incorporating and developing new technological hardware, as well as reconstructing processes (and organization) to ensure competitive use of the new technology. *Reengineering* involves changes in dynamic processes and organizational structure; hence, it represents a subset of transformation. It may involve the destruction or severe downsizing of existing organizations in addition to the coordination of existing organizations through information technology. In the interwar era this most prominently concerned radio, radar, and electro-mechanical tabulation machines. Military reengineering more commonly requires the augmentation of traditional organizations with flexible units specifically designed to shoulder their worst disruptions. *Motorization* refers to the use of internal combustion engines to enhance the mobility of an army, specifically its trucks, motorcycles, and cars. *Armored warfare* involves the use of internal-combustion-powered vehicles designed for combat, including tanks, self-propelled artillery, infantry carriers, and tank destroyers. *Mechanization* denotes the military incorporation of the internal combustion engine in general; it comprises both motorization and armored warfare.

Reengineering is a term coined by Michael Hammer in the late 1980s; it refers to a change in internal business processes to achieve significant increases in performance.[5] By *process,* one may assume problem-solving methodologies in general and their management in particular. To be more specific, it implies the flow of information, constraints, and resources within the organization. As Hammer originally described it, if change is radical, the resulting performance increases can be profound. To borrow his words: "Reengineering is the fundamental rethinking and radical redesign of business processes to achieve dramatic

---

[5] For a review of original and revised concepts, see Paul Bracken, *Reengineering and Information Technology: Relationships and Lessons Learned*, Santa Monica, Calif.: RAND Corporation, unpublished manuscript.

improvements in critical, contemporary measures of performance, such as cost, quality, service, and speed."[6] Hammer originally advocated throwing out all past perceptions of how the business should operate and redesigning it using only current and future considerations—that is, starting over with a "blank sheet." Hammer justified such a revolutionary attitude towards business reengineering by pointing to the need to depart from the traditional business processes based on the division of labor. Great savings and performance enhancements are obtainable if the enterprise will ruthlessly redesign its organization along value-added process lines. Some of the results of reengineering in the 1990s included decentralization, a flattening of corporate hierarchies, the empowering of individual employees with greater managerial responsibilities, and the demand for more critical-thinking skills to integrate traditionally fragmented business processes. In addition, however, there were many bad—and sometimes fatal—side effects as a result of extreme disruption. There is an alternative approach, what is referred to elsewhere[7] as *pragmatic reengineering*, that neither requires nor encourages severe disruptions unless absolutely necessary, and then on a selective basis only. Pragmatic reengineering depends heavily on using information technology to integrate traditionally fractured business processes. There are many parallels with military transformation and its emphasis on, for instance, network-centric operations and common operational pictures.

---

[6] Michael Hammer and James Champy, *Reengineering the Corporation: A Manifesto for Business Revolution*, New York: Harper Business, 1993, p. 32.

[7] See Davis (2001) and Bracken (unpublished).

CHAPTER TWO

Historical Analysis

Incorporating the Internal Combustion Engine Without Reengineering Basic Military Processes

The Italian Military

The Italian experience illustrates how an army with strong economic and military support, as well as a considerable degree of technical expertise in its supporting industries, can nonetheless fail badly by rejecting any serious attempts at reengineering.

The Italian army, or Regio Esercito, of World War II was the least effective force of World War II that conducted major offensive actions. Its inability to defend its interwar conquest of Ethiopia, its disastrous invasion of Greece, its failure to support the flanks of the German Third Army leading to the encirclement at Stalingrad, and the dramatic collapse of its initial invasion of Egypt were the most notable events. The only successful unaided conquest it accomplished was of British Somaliland. Nevertheless, the senior military leadership enjoyed full support from the Fascist regime. In addition to the considerable prestige that these commanders enjoyed as bulwarks of Fascist Italy, they also received opportunities to test combat doctrines and innovations in the colonial campaigns of Libya and Ethiopia, as well as in the Spanish Civil War.

The problem with the Italian army was that it was the quintessential self-serving bureaucracy, dedicated to promoting its internal power and prestige at the expense of operational performance. Such egoism is hardly uncommon among military organizations, however. What made things especially disastrous was the army's inculcation of Fascist

Italy's emphasis of style over substance, as well as its self-serving support for Mussolini's absurd concentration of supreme military control. Any innovation, both technical and organizational, that threatened its shortsighted interests was quickly suppressed, and with little opposition from the Duce. Mussolini, after all, largely retained his mind-set as a public-relations-savvy journalist. He preferred to make ludicrous declarations of Fascist military superiority and fund symbolic displays of military prowess instead of making difficult military modernization choices.[1] He was scarcely a design-obsessed Hitler, who thoroughly enjoyed submerging himself in the details of military developments. The senior Italian army leaders sought to ensure the maximum number of positions for their officer corps to enhance their power, and thus adopted a conservative reading of World War I based on their own immediate experience in the Alpine front against Austria-Hungary. According to this, the primary way to prepare for modern warfare was to focus on the primacy of the infantry armed with rifles and bayonets. Expensive heavy equipment and rigorous doctrinal innovation was not a priority. While the senior commanders did not entirely reject the opportunities suggested by the internal combustion engine in the Great War, they did view such technology with skepticism. The senior commanders pressed far harder for the modernization of their artillery, albeit with little success, than for the development of main battle tanks.[2] Given Italy's industrial and material constraints, not to mention the distraction of Mussolini's imperial campaigns, it was too convenient to conclude that the pursuit of such innovative capital equipment was not cost-effective.

Italy primarily conceded to mechanization during the 1930s by deploying such tankettes as the FIAT-Ansaldo L3/35 and the Carro Veloce 33—suitable only for gunning down lightly armed Africans—and the medium-weight Carro Armato M11/39. The Italian army's focus on quantity rather than quality created a bloated bureaucracy that was dedi-

---

[1] For a revealing examination of the Fascist corruption of the Italian army, see Denis Mack Smith, *Mussolini's Roman Empire*, New York: Viking Press, 1976, pp. 169–89.

[2] MacGregor Knox, *Mussolini Unleashed 1939–1941: Politics and Strategy in Fascist Italy's Last War*, Cambridge: Cambridge University Press, 1982, p. 26.

cated to supplying and training hundreds of thousands of infantrymen, while blocking any ambitious officer or official that pressed for more technically progressive doctrines. That bureaucracy proved notoriously deficient even with the routine supply and training of enlisted infantrymen. Not only did it incorporate new motorized technology and tactics only marginally, it also neglected traditional disciplinary processes that had held the army together following the Caporetto disaster of 1917. A similar tale could be told about the Italian air force, which stubbornly held on to the biplane through the 1930s due to an obsolete notion of tradeoffs between maneuverability and speed. The fascist self-delusion of the Regia Aeronautica even surpassed that of the army.

The output of Italy's armament industry was another matter. Despite material and engineering-manpower shortages, it still managed to learn enough from combat experience to try to overcome the initial inferiority of its designs. The Carro Armato M13/40 performed quite competitively against the British cruiser tanks encountered initially in North Africa. While the Semovente M40 self-propelled gun proved a failure against Russian T-34s and KV-1s, it was effective enough in North Africa when engaging light British tanks. Ironically, the Italians finally started producing a reasonable medium-weight tank, the M15/42, only shortly before their capitulation in 1943. As Mussolini typically complained, after the fact, "We arrive at perfection [only] when it is useless."[3] The Germans quickly incorporated the new Italian tank into their forces and continued employing it through 1944. Italian failure at armored and motorized warfare, therefore, cannot be blamed on their limited industrial and engineering resources.

Other dimensions of the Italians' extreme military conservatism included the army's failure to develop an effective general staff. As Mac-Gregor Knox bluntly stated, "Innovation was and remained suspect, because it meant scrapping a force structure that derived from the army's deeply felt conception of war and directly served the interests of the officer corps."[4] So committed was the Italian officer corps to maintaining its

---

[3] MacGregor Knox, *Hitler's Italian Allies: Royal Armed Forces, Fascist Regime, and the War of 1940–1943*, Cambridge: Cambridge University Press, 2000, p. 65.

[4] Knox, 2000, 55.

traditional military processes that the disastrous defeat of Italian troops at Guadalajara during the Spanish Civil War and their decisive reliance on material superiority in Ethiopia inspired only cosmetic organizational changes in Rome.[5] Nevertheless, individual Italian combat units were capable of adapting, especially when cooperating with German units. If the Italian Army received any admiration during its combat engagements of World War II, beyond its traditional Piedmontese prowess in mountain warfare, it was in learning informally how to fight with combined-arms tactics the rigidly traditional "separate arms" regiments of Great Britain. In doing so it achieved some basic cooperation between tanks, infantry, and artillery units in combat.[6] Effective military reengineering, in short, may or may not be reflected in official doctrine.

In spite of the Italian army's poor performance, Mussolini lavished relatively generous budgets on his military forces. During the latter 1930s, his defense spending approximated France's and Great Britain's, even though national income was less than a quarter of the latter's. On the other hand, Italy spent more than two-thirds of those funds on military actions in Spain and Ethiopia.[7] Those expensive classrooms of modern warfare impressed Italian field commanders, but their sophisticated lessons fell on deaf ears among the high command. Like many other military organizations, the senior Italian generals chose to ignore the evidence that contradicted their self-serving doctrine.

The behavior of the Italian navy differed considerably from that of the army. It focused on capital, rather than human investments. That hardly meant the Italian navy was poorly manned, however. The willingness of its officers and sailors to fight Allied vessels and protect Axis convoys, even when facing virtually suicidal odds, is well established. Their quasi-fanatical dedication to keeping the Africa Korps fueled, even if it meant piling highly explosive gasoline containers on the decks of their warships, speaks for itself. And in spite of the extremely weak air support from the Regia Aeronautica, the Italian navy still managed

---

[5] Knox, 1982, 28–9.

[6] Knox, 2000, 154.

[7] Allan Millett and Williamson Murray, eds., *Military Effectiveness*, Vol. II: *The Interwar Years*, Boston: Allen and Unwin, 1988, p. 170.

to sink over 60 British warships—far more than were sunk by the Japanese navy and the German surface fleet. Before the war, the Italian navy was impressive for its pioneering naval research into radar and its prowess in torpedo technology—the latter resulting in powerful aerial and magnetic torpedoes and contributing to the *maiali*, or small human-guided torpedoes—the ultimate weapons in asymmetric naval warfare. It was with the *maiali* that Italian commandos sunk the British battleships *Valiant* and *Queen Elizabeth* in the harbor of Alexandria, which helped avenge the battleships temporarily sunk at Tarento by the British Swordfish torpedo bombers.[8] Nevertheless, the Italian naval obsession with the traditional battleship doctrine of Mahan ensured its failure to exploit fully such innovations and capabilities early on in the war. The Italian naval experience was yet another example of employing some bold new weaponry but not reengineering the organization or its processes (as evidenced in particular by their failure to develop aircraft carriers, antiaircraft defenses, and radar surveillance).[9] In such cases, the technology can be used, occasionally with stunning success, but its full potential is never reached. Overall, Fascist Italy represented a classic example of the disastrous consequences of adapting new technology without engaging in reengineering.

The British Army

The British Army after World War I faced an entirely different political landscape from the Regio Esercito. While the Italian army enjoyed generous funding and political influence in exchange for its support of the Fascist regime, the British army endured prolonged political hostility. Discredited by antiwar movements for its high casualties on the Western Front, it also endured relatively low levels of funding and popular disarmament campaigns.[10] Only in 1939 was it officially authorized to

---

[8] Marc Antonio Bragadin, *The Italian Navy in World War II*, Annapolis, Md.: United States Naval Institute, 1957, pp. 282–86.

[9] Robert Mallet, *The Italian Navy and Fascist Expansionism 1935–1940*, London: Frank Cass, 1998, p. 172.

[10] Brian Bond, *British Military Policy Between the Two World Wars*, Oxford: Clarendon Press, 1980, p. 35.

resume planning for warfare on the European continent. This followed years of "limited liability" pronouncements in Parliament that the British army would never again fight a major continental war.[11] The army's strength was further dissipated by heavy colonial manpower commitments in Egypt and Palestine, along with the traditional service demands of India. The additional budget cutbacks in response to the Great Depression also restricted its strength. The esprit de corps and deep traditions of the British regiments played an important role in maintaining the morale and cohesion of the army during these grim years, especially in the enlisted ranks. Unfortunately, the anti-intellectual aspects of such a cohesive culture also helped negate the army's seminal innovations in armored warfare: the innovations occurred but were only marginally adopted.

The British were responsible for the original invention and deployment of the tank during the Great War. Starting with a limited trial at the Battle of the Somme in 1916, and continuing with a temporary (albeit unexploited) breakthrough at Cambrai, the newly organized Tank Corps displayed a technical and organizational creativity that the British army had rarely displayed before then. This wartime innovation culminated with a full-scale assault on Amiens in 1918. Unfortunately for the British, mechanical reliability and German resilience in improvising antitank defenses led to irreplaceable losses. By the end of the war, the Tank Corps admitted to having only eight tanks in operation.[12]

This failure of Great Britain to design, manufacture, and deploy tanks with sufficient power to achieve decisive results on the Western Front fueled the heated military debates surrounding tanks during the 1920s. The most famous participants were J. F. C. Fuller and B. H. Liddell Hart, who were among the greatest military intellectuals of the 20th century. Fuller and Hart outlined such essential elements of armored warfare as (1) the synergy of tank and aircraft through close air support, (2) the utility of tanks in attacking command centers and logistical bases rather than "merely" providing close infantry support, and (3) the vast new opportunities for strategies of indirect approach or maneuver.

---

[11] Bond, 1980, p. 176.

[12] Len Deighton, *Blitzkrieg: From the Rise of Hitler to the Fall of Dunkirk*, New York: Alfred A. Knopf, 1979, p. 110.

Unfortunately, Fuller and Hart coupled such intellectual pre-science with increasingly nasty criticism of the British military establishment. So severe did their criticism become during the 1930s that it stimulated a unified reaction by most of the army against armored warfare and its advocates. Given these developments, it is remarkable that a small portion of the British army was nonetheless able—during the late 1920s and early 1930s—to conduct a series of full-scale experiments and demonstrations of mechanized warfare that impressed the world. The experiments were conducted under the leadership of Lord Milne from 1926 to 1934. Armed with a progressive and flexible intellect, Milne's initial experiments demonstrated the decisive superiority that tanks can have over cavalry and infantry—especially in maneuvers. Using the broad Salisbury Plain, these experiments established basic techniques for motorizied infantry and artillery support, as well as maintaining logistical truck networks and utilizing radio communications. Milne's subordinate, General Burnett-Stuart, went on to devise basic tank maneuvers in the desert as the commander of British forces in the Middle East during the early 1930s. Although not as optimistic about armor's capabilities as some, he worked hard to minimize its vulnerabilities.[13] The ultimate compliment paid to such British efforts in both armored doctrinal theory and full-scale maneuver came from the great German general Guderian. While assigned to a motorized logistics command after World War I, he immersed himself in the writings of Fuller and Martel.[14] Later he noted how much his conceptualization of the panzer division depended on Milne's experiments.[15] Marshal Tukhachevsky of the Red Army was similarly influenced by the active armored-warfare investigations in Britain during the 1920s.[16]

---

[13] Harold R. Winton, *To Change an Army: General Sir John Burnett-Stuart and British Armored Doctrine, 1927–1938*, Lawrence: University of Kansas Press, 1988, p. 86.

[14] Anthony John Trythall, *"Boney" Fuller: Soldier, Strategist, and Writer*, New Brunswick, N.J.: Rutgers University Press, 1977, p. 211.

[15] Heinz Guderian, *Panzer Leader*, New York: Ballantine Books, 1957, p. 13.

[16] For Tukhachevsky's introduction to J. F. C. Fuller's *The Reformation of War*, see Richard Simpkin, *Deep Battle: The Brainchild of Marshal Tuckachevskii*, London: Brassey's Defence Publishers, 1987, pp. 125–35. Also see Jacob W. Kipp, "Military Reform and the Red Army, 1918–1941," in Harold R. Winton and David R. Mets, eds., *The Challenge of Change: Military Institutions and New Realities, 1918–1941*, Lincoln: University of Nebraska Press, 2000, pp. 142–43.

As progressive as Milne was, his commitment to armored warfare did not persist with subsequent commanders in chief. Montgomery-Massingberd, while progressive with respect to innovative weapon procurement, remained rigidly conservative when it came to doctrinal issues. He remained convinced that the next continental war would be fought largely along the same lines as the Great War. In response to the impressive performance of the Tank Corps in the 1931 maneuvers, he chose to redirect British military modernization towards a gradual mechanization of the entire British army, but one focused largely on adding trucks without upsetting existing processes. This policy ultimately prevailed during the Great Depression. Montgomery-Massingberd's dedication to minimizing any disturbances to traditional military processes was also reflected in his suppression of the critical army studies of the Great War campaigns, which were finally completed in 1932. Not only did he have offending sections deleted in the drafts released to senior officers, he let it be known in no uncertain terms that disagreement with his policies represented disloyalty, if not insubordination.

The British at least had the good fortune of holding General Martel responsible for tank development, however marginal the support provided to him was. A tank commander from World War I, Martel published treatises on armored warfare and pioneered the lightweight "tankette" to enhance infantry mobility. Impressed with Soviet tank demonstrations in 1936, he enlisted Walter Christie's help from the United States, arranging for the Morris Motors Group to purchase the rights to one of his advanced tank prototypes.[17] This resulted in the introduction of the Cruiser Tank Mk III, the first tank available to the British for strategic long-range actions.

There was, then, some progress. Still, when the Cruiser Tank was introduced in 1937, the British army still lacked a formal tank division, although it had finally succeeded in convincing the cavalry forces to exchange its horses for lightweight reconnaissance tanks. A mobile division was authorized for Egypt, and the leading tank reformer, Hobart, was sent to command it. Unfortunately, he encountered so much

---

[17] Charles Messenger, *The Blitzkrieg Story*, New York: Charles Scribner's Sons, 1976, p. 109.

opposition from senior commanders that he left Egypt in disgrace by 1939. As a consequence, Britain entered World War II with only two armored divisions available for action in France—one of which was too poorly trained to be used effectively. The vast majority of British tanks were dispersed ineffectually in smaller infantry-support units.[18]

In spite of the experimental and strategic creativity of its leading military minds, the British army did little to overturn the anti-intellectualism and lack of disinterested professionalism that permeated the traditional regimental culture. This was manifested by its unwillingness to develop and adopt effective combined-arms techniques.[19] Infighting among the armored-warfare advocates compounded problems, as did the absence of a strategic vision. Nevertheless, as Williamson Murray concluded, it was ultimately the British army's inability to learn from hard-won experience that lay at the heart of Britain's missed opportunities with armored warfare.[20] Having dissipated the officers responsible for the innovative armor experiments throughout the army during the late 1930s, and having ensured that none received senior commands during World War II, the British army had to suffer on the battlefield for ignoring the lessons that it taught so well to the Germans and Russians before the war. The different British arms were persistently unable to achieve effective combat coordination throughout the war, especially with respect to armored warfare. Unlike the Italian infantry divisions that quickly learned from the Germans how to forge effective cooperation between armor, infantry, and artillery, the British persisted with all-tank operations.[21]

---

[18] Messenger, 1976, p. 113.

[19] For an in-depth analysis of the deep dysfunctions of the British Army during World War II, including their weakness in combined-arms techniques, see Timothy Harrison Place, *Military Training in the British Army, 1940–1944: From Dunkirk to D-Day*, London: Frank Cass, 2000.

[20] William Murray and Alan Millet, eds., *Military Innovation in the Interwar Period*, Cambridge: Cambridge University Press, 1996, p. 29.

[21] The theory supporting all-tank operations was actually a legacy of Fuller. Although most of Fuller's ideas were excellent, he failed to understand the need to supplement tanks with infantry and artillery, especially when facing powerful antitank weaponry in the hands of infantry forces.

The U.S. Army

During the interwar era, the U.S. Army suffered neither from the severe industrial and material resource constraints of the Italians nor from the vituperative antiwar discourse of the British. It was also spared the heavy imperialistic commitments that drained both of those forces in the 1930s. The U.S. Army had potential access to the greatest automobile industry in the world, as well as enormous reservoirs of engineering, scientific, and educational talent. It also boasted an Ordnance Corps that established a crucial foundation for modern industrial production: the "Armory System" of interchangeable-part production. Coupled with the fact that officer education was grounded by the engineering orientation of West Point, the U.S. Army seemingly had all the necessary economic and intellectual resources to be in the front ranks of military motorized and armored warfare.

Yet such leadership was not manifested during the interwar era. During the late 19th and early 20th centuries, when the United States transformed itself from an agrarian into a heavily industrialized country, the U.S. Army was increasingly dominated by semiromantic, antimodern officers with almost aristocratic pretensions. The officer corps' cultural attachment to polo and equestrian arts speaks for itself. (Patton's insistence on wearing his jodhpurs through the end of World War II is also revealing.) The industrialized warfare the Army pioneered during the Civil War was eroded by years of frontier-security duties against Native Americans and Mexicans. The embarrassing performance of its weaponry in the Spanish American War, and its utter dependence on the Allies for both heavy and small arms during World War I, underscores this point.[22]

Following the vast mobilization and equally rapid demobilization associated with the Great War, the Army's primary concern was to maintain the integrity of its officer corps. Like their Italian counterparts, the Army's leaders consequently sought to maximize the number of soldiers in its ranks to help preserve the command structures.

---

[22] For a detailed description of the sheer incompetence of the U.S. Ordnance Department with respect to small arms during the Spanish American War and World War I, see William H. Hallahan, *Misfire: The Story of How America's Small Arms Have Failed Our Military*, New York: Charles Scribner's Sons, 1994, pp. 233–349.

Unfortunately for them, no American Mussolini appeared to gratify their desire. The Army never obtained its "minimum" demand for a peacetime force of almost 300,000 troops, as Congress had authorized in 1920. Subsequent budget cuts left it with a force of 14,000 officers and approximately 100,000 soldiers—even before the commencement of the Great Depression. This placed it near the level of the German Reichswehr following the Treaty of Versailles. As a consequence, any proposals for innovative applications of the internal combustion engine represented an implicit threat to the Army's perceived core interest in maintaining its skeletal structure.[23] Given the choice between maintaining the officer ranks and paying for new machinery, Army chiefs of staff invariably selected the former. Not unlike the senior command of the Regio Esercito, the U.S. Army leadership remained committed to the premise that the industrialization of warfare had not altered the primacy of massed infantry or the need for horses.[24] The tendency of the U.S. Army Air Corps and Corps of Engineers to siphon off the most technologically talented officers, as well as the 1920 law passed by Congress that eliminated a separate Tank Corps only enhanced this trend. Armored warfare thus remained within the domain of the conservative Infantry command, where the tank would be treated solely as an auxiliary weapon until 1940.

Interestingly, such hostility to modern engineering processes did not extend to broader strategic concerns. Given the dismal coordination of the Ordnance Office and heavy commercial industry in World War I, the U.S. Army founded the Army Industrial College in 1924. Its extensive surveys of American industrial capacity would serve as blueprints for the military transformation of commercial production in World War II. It was the U.S. Army's concern for such strategic issues that proved to be its saving grace in World War II. Its persistent

---

[23] David E. Johnson, *Fast Tanks and Heavy Bombers: Innovation in the U.S. Army, 1917–1945*, Ithaca, N.Y.: Cornell University Press, 1998, p. 71.

[24] This doctrinal commitment to infantry is reflected in the official post–World War I manual *FSR 1923*. The same focus persisted in the next major revision, *FSR 1939*. For a detailed analysis of the stagnation of U.S. Army doctrine between the wars, see William O. Odom, *After the Trenches: The Transformation of U.S. Army Doctrine, 1918–1939*, College Station: Texas A&M University Press, 1999.

failure to defeat German forces on equal terms became moot, given the United States' vastly superior industrial and logistical base, which ensured decidedly unequal terms.

To return to the story of armored warfare: the United States was not lacking in talent. Walter Christie, for example, was perhaps the most creative tank designer in the interwar era. His pioneering designs for high-speed light tanks included sophisticated suspension systems and powerful engines. The Army also had highly capable officers within its ranks, such as George Patton, who commanded a tank brigade during World War I, and Dwight Eisenhower, who quickly grasped the revolutionary strategic implications of armored warfare in the early 1920s. With Major Bradford Chynoweth, the U.S. Army had an equally perceptive tank officer who easily saw past the technical limitations of World War I tanks. He recognized the challenges to Army processes that their inevitable progress represented, including the obsolescence of horse cavalry.[25] The interwar U.S. Army also profited from the senior management of Secretary of War Dwight Davis and, to a lesser extent, Army Chief of Staff Charles Summerall. They were particularly impressed with the British armored warfare experiments of the late 1920s. In response, they established the innovative, albeit short-lived, "Mechanized Force." Finally, there were cavalry officers, such as Colonel Edmunds and General Chaffee, who maintained that reconnaissance and long-range raids behind enemy lines were their ultimate missions, not horseback riding. There were also many perceptive American officers who rejected the mechanized-artillery theories—supposedly implied by the Spanish Civil War and championed by General McNair—that antitank destroyers were the most effective means of stopping tank offenses. General Devers, after taking command of the Armored Force in 1940, correctly anticipated American combat realities by vehemently rejecting arguments that tank-versus-tank combat was too expensive, inefficient, and avoidable.[26] Again, the U.S. Army was not lacking in individual talent or interest in armored warfare.

---

[25] Johnson, 1998, p. 74.

[26] Johnson, 1998, p. 152.

Unfortunately, the institutional structure of the U.S. Army inhibited effective use of its intellectual assets in this area. A number of organizational constraints prevented the Army from obtaining a competitive armor doctrine and organization. The maintenance of a decentralized command structure, where considerable authority was invested in the individual service chiefs, was one problem. Service chiefs effectively ruled as feudal lords over the Infantry, Artillery, and Cavalry branches, as well as the Signal, Ordnance, and Engineering Corps. This gave them the power to resist or shape any motorization opportunities that undermined their branch's immediate interests. Infantry chiefs such as Robert Allen, Stephen Fuqua, Malin Craig, and George Lunch strenuously upheld the doctrine in which infantry is primary, with tanks useful only in an auxiliary role. They strenuously objected to any attempt to establish an independent tank arm, such as the Mechanized Force of 1930–31. They also pointed to improvements in antitank weaponry as justification for keeping tanks wedded to an infantry-support role.

Cavalry chiefs such as Leon Kromer did acknowledge the enormous strategic implications that mechanization offered the cavalry, but they continued to argue for the tactical utility of the horse.[27] Moreover, Chaffee and other pro-armor cavalry officers only proposed an armored cavalry doctrine that preserved the traditional cavalry processes of reconnaissance and raiding. Kromer's replacement, John Herr, went one step further by insisting that cavalry mechanization would be tolerated only if there were a corresponding increase in horsemen. The active resistance of the service chiefs to block any threat to their narrow service interests, even after the early Blitzkrieg triumphs of 1939–40, led General Marshall to ruthlessly centralize the U.S. Army in 1942.[28]

Even more destructive than the external relations of the Army's service chiefs were their internal policies. During the interwar era, they had a quasi-dictatorial intolerance to subordinates who contributed to

---

[27] Johnson, 1998, p. 135.

[28] It is worth noting here how easily one can learn the wrong lesson from a case history. The problem Marshall faced was not decentralized command per se, but decentralized command populated by leaders resistant to a unified Army vision. In other circumstances, the creativity of decentralized commanders can *facilitate* innovation. Also, decentralization can mitigate the excesses of foolish top leaders. In short, contextual details do matter.

any published discourse that questioned established service doctrine. General Farnsworth, for example, threatened Captain Eisenhower with a court-martial in the early 1920s for insubordination. Eisenhower had published an article arguing how progress in tank technology would invariably lead to the obsolescence of existing infantry doctrine. Likewise, virtually no articles critical of the primacy of infantry, and the correspondingly secondary role of tanks, appeared in military publications throughout much of the 1920s.[29] Similar intolerance confronted any cavalry officer who dared to suggest that horsemen were obsolete. The exhaustive arguments Patton made on behalf of the horseman when he abandoned the Tank Corps to return to the cavalry, followed by his subsequent promotions, suggest the benefits of such conformity. He still argued after the fall of Poland, for example, that a properly led and heavily equipped horse-cavalry force could repel an armored assault.[30] By contrast, based on their experimental maneuvers through the early 1930s, both the French and the German cavalry forces soberly concluded that they needed to replace horses with as many motorized vehicles as possible, especially light reconnaissance tanks. They sought to maintain their traditional reconnaissance duties while eliminating the confusion and needless complexity that horses increasingly represented for modern tactics. In Patton's and Herr's defense, however, the Americans—unlike the French and Germans—worried about the vast tracts of rugged mountainous deserts along the Mexican border, where paved roads were nonexistent and where tanks dared not tread.

The organization of mechanized warfare in the United States also suffered from corrosive relations between Infantry and supportive organizations such as the Ordnance Department and Army Corps of Engineers. One of the reasons the Mechanized Force failed to win much support was the dismal performance of the obsolete World War I tanks that comprised the majority of its force. The only new tanks acquired were a few Christie prototypes. This lack of progress was not entirely due to the plethora of World War I tanks, nor to a frugal Congress. Throughout

---

[29] Johnson, 1998, p. 76.

[30] John Daley, "Patton Versus the 'Motor Maniacs': An Interwar Defense of Horse Cavalry," *Armor*, Vol. 106, No. 2, 1997, p. 13.

the 1920s, a continuous conflict existed between Infantry and Ordnance due to the engineers' dictum that no tanks exceed 15 tons. The senior engineering officers pointed to the weight limit of their portable bridges. This constraint was coupled with the traditional Ordnance attitude that close involvement of combat commanders in weapons development only lengthens procurement time. Consequently, there was a consistent failure to furnish suitable tanks.[31] Designing a tank with sufficient armor, firepower, and power to meet Infantry-branch requirements proved impossible for inexperienced Ordnance engineers to execute when subject to the 15-ton weight restriction. The Ordnance Department was also notorious for its intolerance of Christie's eccentricities and the supposed design flaws of his cutting-edge tanks. As a consequence, Ordnance succeeded in convincing Infantry to accept its inferior T-5 Combat Car in 1934 and reject Christie's vastly superior T-4 design.[32]

Like the British army, which suffered throughout World War II for its failure to overcome a deep-seated regimental myopia that resisted change, the U.S. Army also paid a price for its maintenance of a decentralized organizational structure throughout the interwar era. Marshall's reorganization effort in 1942, under the strain of never-ending Japanese victories in the Pacific, failed to dislodge the parochial attitudes of many senior Army officers. General Lesley McNair, for example, strongly advocated and ultimately developed mechanized tank-destroyer forces. Especially controversial was his theory that they be held in reserve against a massed panzer breakthrough. His view, stereotypical of an artillery officer, saw tank destroyers as an armored-warfare extension of the artillery's traditional functions. McNair convinced Marshall, with commendable economic reasoning, to prevent an expensive tank from performing like a cheap gun system. Such reasoning paralleled the traditional doctrine of prohibiting Infantry from pursuing what artillery can accomplish with far less risk. Nevertheless, the lightly armored and partially enclosed tank destroyers proved to be poor defenses against German panzers.[33] In addition, infantry units

---

[31] Johnson, 1998, p. 79.

[32] George F. Hofmann, "Combatant Arms vs. Combined Arms: The U.S. Army's Quest for Deep Offensive Operations and an Operational Level of Warfare," *Armor*, Vol. 106, No. 1, 1997, pp. 9–10.

rebelled at the prospect of going into combat while the tank destroyers waited passively in the rear. Consequently, they were rapidly employed as assault guns, whose effectiveness (and vulnerability) Lieuten-
ant Audie Murphy demonstrated by single-handedly killing over 240
Germans in 1944.

Many senior American tank commanders insisted on keeping the
M4 Sherman tank throughout the war as the main battle tank, in spite
of its manifest inferiority relative to the heavy Panther and Tiger tanks
developed for the Eastern Front. This betrayed a cavalry mind-set that
favored maneuverability and durability over firepower and survivabil-
ity. At least the Sherman represented a real improvement over the light
M3 tank that the Army deployed initially. (Soviet tankers nicknamed
it the "coffin," given the internal explosive effect that occurred when an
antitank round sheared its rivets.) The Soviet army, likewise, generally
restricted the M4 Sherman to close infantry support.

The U.S. Army certainly demonstrated remarkable strengths. It
developed a far greater capacity to engage in combined-arms operations than the British, especially with respect to coordinated artillery
assaults. Its ability to expand rapidly in terms of forces and industrial
support, beginning in 1940, revealed exceptional organizational ability. The Army also mastered the procurement of the most innovative, if
not durable, transportation vehicles during the war. These included the
jeep, the DUKW (or amphibious truck), the virtually indestructible
2.5-ton truck, and the all-terrain half-tracks. Such equipment permitted the U.S. armored divisions to transport all their troops in vehicles
that were both armored and capable of off-road mobility—something
no other army could claim. Nevertheless, the Army failed to wage continuous campaigns of annihilation against the German forces in defending Western Europe, especially in Italy and the German border
region. It could never boast the ruthless liquidation of entire German
divisions, if not armies, as the Soviet's demonstrated on such a colos-
sal scale in Operation Bagration (1944). This revealed a weakness of
American armored doctrines that combat experience, logistical coordi-

---

[33] Geoffrey Perret, *There's a War to Be Won: The U.S. Army in World War II*, New York: Random
House, 1991, pp. 105–6.

nation, and even massive air support could not offset. The legacy of the interwar failure to reconcile a cavalry and infantry orientation towards armored warfare was ultimately reflected by the bitter attritional warfare that the Germans inflicted, particularly with their heavy panzers and devastating antitank guns. Such a legacy would persist until the U.S. Army's conceptual transformation, which began in the late 1970s and resulted in the AirLand Battle doctrine. Only then did the Army finally start comprehending Soviet-style Operational Art and ultimately mastered "shock-inducing" maneuver operations, as demonstrated in both of the wars against Iraq.

Incorporating the Internal Combustion Engine and Changing Basic Military Processes, but for Fallacious Reasons

The French Army

The French army in the interwar era provides a sober lesson in military reengineering. Here was an organization that managed to produce the most technologically advanced armored forces in the world and to employ the internal combustion engine in innovative new ways. It was willing to reengineer itself fundamentally in accordance with combat-forged doctrines, and it received generous funding and political support. Even Winston Churchill proclaimed the French army "the most perfectly trained and faithful mobile force in Europe" shortly before World War II.[34] Nevertheless, the French army endured the most rapid military collapse of any great power during the 20th century. Military transformations can provide powerful results—but only if the new processes reengineered are relevant.

During the interwar era, the French army consciously transformed itself in response to the new weaponry, heavy casualties, and economic mobilization of World War I. Both soldiers and civilians were appalled at the pointless bloodletting caused by the aggressive of-

---

[34] Robert A. Doughty, "The French Armed Forces," in Allan Millet and Williamson Murray, eds., *Military Effectiveness*, Vol. II: *The Interwar Era*, Boston: Allen and Unwin, 1988, p. 39.

fensive tactics of the initial campaigns. The frontal assaults against German positions in the first month of war alone cost over 100,000 French lives.[35] The French were equally impressed with the heavy casualties they succeeded in inflicting on the German infantry assaults at Verdun, when they relied on stubborn defensive tactics. In the offenses under Marshal Pétain in 1917, the French finally came to appreciate well-coordinated tactics that rested heavily on concentrated artillery fire and minimized exposure to infantry.[36] They also relied on incremental advances coupled with consolidation using strong defensive positions, as well as synchronized coordination with heavy artillery fire (including creeping barrages). These approaches demanded centralized control over the battlefield, yet they succeeded in maximizing the lethality of the new rapid-fire artillery and machine guns, while minimizing exposure. Unlike the British, who considered the trench warfare of the Western Front an aberration (as one senior British officer supposedly said, "Thank God the war is over so we can get back to real soldiering"), the French were dedicated to transforming themselves rationally in response to their experience. In their eyes, the artillery, machine guns, and vast national mobilization effort of World War I represented a major military revolution that made all previous doctrines obsolete. The French thus reversed their aggressive offensive doctrines of 1914 to institutionalize their decisive methodical techniques of 1918.

Focusing on its victory in the Great War, the French command sponsored a series of in-depth analyses of its conduct. The result was formulated as the artillery-centric doctrine of Methodical Battle.[37] The dominant power of modern weaponry, they concluded, lay not in maneuver, but in firepower. Only through the close coordination of infantry and artillery forces under centralized control could enemy forces be destroyed while husbanding one's own forces. This did not

---

[35] John Mosier, *The Myth of the Great War: A New Military History of World War I*, New York: Harper Collins, 2001, p. 72.

[36] Mosier, 2001, pp. 278–280.

[37] See the chapter entitled "Firepower and the Methodical Battle" in Robert Allan Doughty, *The Seeds of Disaster: The Development of French Army Doctrine, 1919–1939*, Hamden, Conn.: Archon, 1985, pp. 91–111. Much of the following discussion of the French army in the interwar era is based on this monograph.

mean that defensive strategies alone should be employed. Effective offensive action, however, could only occur after the enemy had been
withered under the full force of firepower. Marshal Pétain pioneered
this process, and Gamelin, the commander in chief during the 1930s,
thoroughly indoctrinated the French army with it. The Maginot Line
resulted from the combined logic of Methodical Battle and the distress-
ing problem of the close proximity of France's most strategic resources
to the German border.[38] By employing advanced reinforced-concrete
designs, a pressurization system to block poison gas attacks, and mutu-
ally supporting networks of casemated artillery and machine guns, the
Maginot Line represented the state of the art in static defensive systems. It also employed generators powered by diesel engines to furnish
a self-contained electrical power network. Such engineering rendered
each fortress capable of withstanding the heaviest and lengthiest sieges
imaginable. The fact that the Germans failed to capture these heavy
fortresses during the Blitzkrieg assault in 1940, having penetrated only
a few of the minor positions, speaks for the French army's ability to
use the internal combustion engine effectively—at least in positional
warfare. That the Germans borrowed many innovations of the Maginot Line in constructing the Atlantic Wall, from 1942 to 1944, speaks
for itself. Financial, strategic, and diplomatic considerations, however,
prevented the French from expanding this fortification network along
the Belgium border all the way to the Atlantic—the traditional invasion route into France. Intent on defending this gap, Pétain, Gamelin,
and the French General Staff formulated the doctrine of Methodical
Battle for the field armies.

The French army took seriously the implications of the tank for
field warfare. They devoted more attention to analyzing new weaponry, including tanks, than virtually any other army during the interwar era.[39] During the 1920s, they engaged in numerous studies
of light and heavy tanks, having concluded that it was impossible to

---

[38] For an in-depth discussion of the political and strategic considerations surrounding the construction of the Maginot Line, see Martin Alexander, *The Republic in Danger: General Maurice
Gamelin and the Politics of French Defence, 1933–1940*, Cambridge, Mass.: Cambridge University Press, 1992, pp. 172–81.

[39] Doughty, 1985, p. 5.

design an "all-purpose" tank. The French army also had an innovative tank leader in General Jean B. Estienne. He played a key role in the innovation of the tank in France during World War I and consistently argued for the development of an independent tank force to exploit the tank's full strategic potential. A long-range, medium-weight tank, he concluded, was essential for this mission. Unfortunately for France, Estienne's authority as tank inspector became subordinate to the Infantry Chief when the Tank Corps was absorbed. He consequently had relatively little bureaucratic power to execute his arguments. By the early 1930s, nonetheless, the French army was sponsoring systematic tests and experiments of tank tactics. The tank's limited perspective of the battlefield, as well as its vulnerability to infantry countermeasures, encouraged the senior French command to dismiss Estienne's arguments. Additional tests in 1933 seemed to prove conclusively that tanks could operate only with strong artillery and infantry support. The increasing performance of antitank weaponry during the 1930s only enhanced this perception of the tank's ancillary role. As a consequence, the tank did little to overturn the Methodical Battle process during the 1930s.

French infantry officers continued to advocate the utility of tanks for close infantry support and increasing the tempo of a centrally controlled battle. This unwillingness to detach tanks from infantry battalions was partially based on the plethora of light Renault Ft-17 tanks from World War I, as well as its replacement, the Renault R-35. Because it failed to procure sufficient numbers of B-1 battle tanks, the French infantry was unable to recognize the potential of an independent tank division. Nevertheless, senior officers such as Gamelin simply failed to entertain the possibility that tanks could restore significant degrees of mobility to the battlefield. The limited maneuvers he authorized were not designed to test the validity of a doctrinal theory. Instead, they tended to serve more as training exercises for conscripted troops. So dogmatic was the doctrine of Methodical Battle that prescriptions such as General Héring's, which argued that armored units should not be "obliged to advance in successive jumps according to classic process of slow attacks based on the movement of infantry and artillery," were not taken seriously until the invasion of Poland in 1939.[40]

In spite of the rigidity of their military doctrine in the 1930s, the French did manage to develop capable tanks, as well as independent tank divisions. The B-1 heavy tank, for all its procurement problems, offered many modern features, including self-sealing petrol tanks, an electric starter, and a gyroscopic compass—not to mention a generous distribution of armor that suited the French respect for the lethality of firepower. Its follow-on, the B-1 bis, boasted a 75-mm gun that could knock out any German tank in service during the late 1930s. It was the remarkably progressive French cavalry, however, that conducted the tests and studies, resulting in the S-35—the best overall tank of the 1940 campaign. Given its relative detachment from the strict army doctrine, the cavalry quickly embraced the concept of a mechanized division centered on the medium weight S-35. It featured the first all-cast hull and turret construction, a 47-mm gun mounted on an electrically control turret, and curved armor to deflect shots. The fact that the Germans incorporated virtually all the French tanks into their service following the 1940 campaign—even the old FT series for military-police work—attests to the excellent tank designs of the French. Unfortunately for France, those armored cavalry units were tied up in screening the army's movement into Belgium when the German breakthrough at Sedan occurred.

France's central impediments included its rigid doctrine and its command structure, which undermined critical thinking within the officer corps. To its credit, such rigidity reflected the pressures of maintaining a combat-ready force composed largely of conscripted soldiers subject to short enlistments. Gamelin's unwillingness to tolerate substantive debate among senior officers concerning Methodical Battle did not help, nor did the popular French political assumption of equating professional mechanized armies with Fascist, antidemocratic aspirations. Such intolerance was compounded by the obsession of French military publications and military academies with analyzing the French campaigns of World War I, to the exclusion of the relatively mobile

---

[40] Doughty, 1985, p. 167.

campaigns conducted in the Middle Eastern and Eastern fronts. Although colonial campaigns were acknowledged, virtually no battles were analyzed that differed significantly from the conditions of the Western Front.[41] This avoidance of substantive historical analysis as France transformed its doctrine reflected a complete rejection of the pre-1914 era, when the French military was obsessed with maneuver and offensive action. That obsession, ironically, had come from *overemphasizing* historical analysis to the exclusion of technical considerations and deductive reasoning. The French army fell into the trap of moving from one extreme doctrinal position to another, based on universalizing the lessons of essentially one campaign.

Late in the game, following the invasion of Poland, the French senior command did learn, unlike the U.S. Infantry and Cavalry chiefs, who still resisted the call for independent armored divisions. The French command reacting by quickly authorizing a panicked construction of two heavy-tank divisions for strategic action along German lines. For the French, however, the eight months between the collapse of Poland and the May 1940 campaign proved far too short for effective reengineering. Given the years of focus on close infantry support, they were quickly outmaneuvered by the German panzer divisions, despite their superior hardware.

Naval and Air Power

The French army was not the only force to discover the errors of its ways—after having *both* assimilated the internal combustion engine *and* reengineered its traditional military processes. However impressive the Allied and Axis navies were in developing aircraft and submarines during the interwar era, the traditional battleship still overshadowed these new technologies. Moffett and Yamamoto worked to incorporate aviation into the command structure of their respective naval establishments and to enhance the technical capability of aircraft carriers and aircraft. In spite of these investments, the navies continued to view such reengineering accomplishments as ancillary to the battleship. The same could be said for submarines. Although the German submarine forces functioned as commerce raiders in World War I, their strategic

---

[41] Doughty, 1985, pp. 75–76.

advantage as independent forces operating away from the focal battle fleet was largely ignored. Even the interwar German navy made the construction of new battleships and cruisers a higher priority than submarines. At that time, the Caribbean maneuvers conducted by the U.S. Navy justified this trend: they supposedly demonstrated the vulnerability of naval aircraft to battleship action, as well as the vulnerability of submarines to both air attack and acoustic sensors of destroyers.

Navies, like armies, tend to showcase experimental outcomes and actual experiences that reinforce their traditional processes. The capital ships of the Royal Navy during World War I not only failed to destroy the German navy when given the opportunity at Jutland, but their need for protection also prevented the British from sending off existing destroyers to safeguard convoys. Likewise, the German battleships proved strategically useless throughout the war. Nevertheless, European navies were building battleships and heavy cruisers with abandon: by 1937, the British and Germans were constructing five each, and the French and Italian, four each.[42]

The hurdles to reengineering basic naval combat processes became boldly apparent after Pearl Harbor in 1941. In spite of the power displayed by their aircraft carriers, the Japanese never assembled a carrier task force of that size again during World War II. Midway was supposed to have been a battle in which the battleship would triumph. The Japanese likewise refused to acknowledge the battleship's obsolescence, attributing their victory at Pearl Harbor to sinking battleships, while neglecting the aircraft carriers and repair facilities.[43] The same could be said for the Americans, who believed that Pearl Harbor was a great military disaster, rather than the tragic, yet convenient, disposal of obsolete technology. In the entire Pacific War, battleships would engage in only four ship-to-ship hostilities. Even in providing fire support for the Marines, the battleship was in some respects a hindrance: the fear of hostile fortress fire, the difficulty of engaging in precision gunnery during high-speed maneuvers, and the awkwardness of highly explo-

---

[42] Robert L. O'Connell, *Sacred Vessels: The Cult of the Battleship and the Rise of the U.S. Navy*, Boulder, Colo.: Westview Press, 1991, p. 304.

[43] O'Connell, 1991, p. 315.

sive ordnance led many naval officers to dismiss the amphibious assault process as impractical. Yet resistance to reengineering fleet processes persisted as the American and Japanese navies were slow in redirecting their submarines away from the close-combat support of battleships and toward strategic independent action, especially commerce raiding. Nonetheless, change eventually did occur with this marginalized technology. After an enormous reengineering effort (which included the relief of almost one-third of the submarine command officers in 1942), the U.S. Navy overcame the timid prewar doctrine, which assumed the submarine was extremely vulnerable.[44] Similarly, the interwar navies proved willing to reengineer numerous subprocesses involving antiaircraft defense and radar surveillance; however, they ultimately moved towards only making incremental amendments to the battleship-fleet doctrine, not towards reengineering themselves around the aircraft carrier. Yet to their credit, the U.S. Navy had conducted numerous studies, and it had assimilated enough naval aviation into their command structure to successfully reengineer its fleets around the carrier just in time for the Battle of Coral Sea.

The U.S. Navy and Army Air Corps, nevertheless, were unprepared for the Japanese Zero fighter. This was the product of the Japanese navy's high-stakes gamble on the ability of the Mitsubishi Corporation to synthesize in one aircraft the seemingly impossible demands for a long-range bomber escort and a maneuverable carrier fighter. Even its project manager, Jiro Horikoshi, lacked confidence in his design team's capacity to fulfill such requirements until well into the detailed design process, despite breakthroughs in driving down the factor of safety in the structural design, introducing an elastic response to the control system, and employing drop tanks.[45] When the final design emerged, however, the Japanese navy had a fighter that outclassed any in the United States. The Japanese demonstrated this soon after Pearl Harbor by annihilating American air power in the Philippines, with absurdly

---

[44] Stephen Peter Rosen, *Winning the Next War: Innovation and the Modern Military*, Ithaca, N.Y.: Cornell University Press, 1991, p. 142.

[45] Jiro Horikoshi, *Eagles of Mitsubishi: The Story of the Zero Fighter*, Seattle: University of Washington Press, 1981, pp. 36–41, 72–80.

few losses. Their willingness to tolerate risky technical proposals was also reflected in their innovative aerial torpedo designs that devastated the battleships at Pearl Harbor, in spite of the shallow depths, and the superior night-fighting capabilities of their surface fleet, as demonstrated at Guadalcanal. The Imperial navy's amphibious warfare capabilities were the most effective in the world. Japan's rapid assaults throughout the Pacific in late 1941 and early 1942 boldly showcased this superiority. It is important to note, however, that the ability of the U.S. Marines Corps to quickly catch up and surpass the Japanese did not come from a hurried effort to emulate them. Instead, the Marines' rapid ascent up the amphibious assault learning curve resulted from their own doctrinal and experimental developments beginning in the early 1920s.

Finally, there is the example of the kamikaze attacks at Okinawa. The difficulty of shooting down a determined pilot who is flying straight into a ship was obvious enough. Less obvious was the utility of a plane-launched, rocket-driven Okha bomb that was piloted by a human operator. Its high speed proved virtually impossible for naval gunners to track. None of this came easily: the Japanese navy had invested heavily in creating a substantial research and development (R&D) infrastructure to minimize the risk of such bold innovations. Its intensive testing and training within the context of carrier warfare reflected that investment, however pointless such military innovations ultimately proved to be in 1945. Such prowess at incorporating devastatingly effective technology, however, could not compensate for the Imperial Navy's fatal reluctance to abandon their outmoded strategic doctrines.

The U.S. Army Air Corps

The British and American air forces of the interwar era were among the most enthusiastic proponents of the internal combustion engine. They advocated its incorporation not only for new military hardware but also for the revolutionary process of strategic bombing. As their disappointing performance in World War II revealed, however, their primary accomplishment between the wars was to secure relatively autonomous status from the ground forces. They formally rejected close combat support as too dangerous and ineffectual relative to strategic bombing. In actuality, such combined-arms action heightened their institutional fear of serving only as an auxiliary service for ground forces. Strategic bombing, in contrast, justified the air-force ambition for organizational autonomy. In short, the enormous effort expended during the interwar era on developing the processes required for strategic bombing seemed motivated more by independent bureaucratic power than objective combat capabilities.

The U.S. Army Air Corps was quite effective in forging new processes in terms of procuring innovative aircraft, gaining effective political support, and conceiving entirely new combat missions. Thanks to their exemption from the traditional ordnance regulations of military procurement and their turn toward the civilian aircraft industry and National Advisory Committee for Aeronautics (NACA), the Army Air Corps received up-to-date aircraft that reflected its ambitions.[46] Equally innovative was its sophistication in securing congressional funding and broad public support. Added to that, General Billy Mitchell was a master of public relations. He demonstrated this by violating the Navy's rules to heighten the drama of the *Ostfriesland* bombing and then by performing mock air raids on New York and Annapolis. His carefully constructed media image of a progressive David fighting against entrenched bureaucratic Goliaths was another tactic that won broad popular support for his vision of strategic air power. By cooperating, if not competing, with the Navy in coastal-defense duties, the Army Air Corps also attempted to whittle down Congress's mistrust of its blatantly offensive military orientation. Its arguments that strategic bombing would reduce the length and cost of war, and that its precision-bombing tactics would reduce civilian casualties, proved convincing to Franklin Delano Roosevelt during the early war years when a land-based assault on the European continent was infeasible.

The procurement of the B-17 bomber in 1937 virtually silenced the Air Corps' in-house critics of strategic bombing. The astonishing long range, high speed, and heavy defensive armaments of that innovative Boeing creation, coupled with the sophisticated Norden bomb-

---

[46] Thomas L. McNaugher, *New Weapons Old Politics: America's Military Procurement Muddle*, Washington, D.C.: Brookings Institution, 1989, pp. 22–23.

sight, were hard to dismiss. The strategic bombing advocates used it to undercut Claire Chennault and others who questioned fundamental assumptions about the relative weakness of air defense systems. By 1937, it became virtually dogmatic that tight formations of heavy bombers could penetrate antiaircraft artillery defenses, locate targets, and deliver sufficient bombs to destroy them while also defeating pursuit aircraft without fighter escorts. The marginal effect of strategic bombing in China and Spain, and the ability of British fighters to inflict heavy losses on German bombers during the Battle of Britain, did little to shake confidence. Hap Arnold had demonstrated in the mid-1930s, after all, that close formations of 40 bombers could hit battleship-sized targets when their bombs were released simultaneously from high altitudes—although only when targets were clearly outlined in perfect weather conditions.[47]

The actual combat experience of the Army Air Corps revealed how poorly prepared it was in confronting a real bombing campaign against a determined enemy. Although initially successful in striking targets and minimizing losses against German fighters when conducting short-range missions over France, it suffered ruinous casualties when conducting deeper missions into Germany by 1943. The problem of confronting German fighters armed with long-range cannons and rockets, along with radar-based ground control systems, proved especially perplexing given the Air Corps' prewar neglect to develop fighter-escort processes.[48] The weakness to the Norden bombsight when subject to poor visibility also rendered the corps' prewar doctrine of daytime precision bombing bankrupt. Its fortune only began to change with the Luftwaffe's decision to concentrate interceptors by 1944 in Germany proper.[49] Bomber-escort fighters no longer had to engage so close to their bases and release their full fuel tanks, thus curtailing their escort mission. But the damage of relying on the prewar

---

[47] Stephen L. McFarland, *America's Pursuit of Precision Bombing, 1910–1945*, Washington, D.C.: Smithsonian Institution Press, 1995, p. 96.

[48] Johnson, 1998, p. 209.

[49] Rosen, 1991, pp. 174–78.

concept of operations was already done, in that thousands of aircraft and flight crews had been lost.

A final irony existed in the development of strategic-bombing processes during the 1920s and 1930s. Both the Royal Air Force (RAF) and the Army Air Corps took their ability to select relevant targets for granted. Intelligence sources would, of course, furnish accurate data as to the location of strategic industries. Bomber training involved little more than learning how to recognize transportation chokepoints and industrial concentrations. Unfortunately, the problem of target allocation became acute during World War II because of the limited economic data available on German industrial operations.[50] The costly bombing campaign to strike the ball-bearing factories of Schweinfurt, for example, had little lasting effect. The Germans already were dispersing strategic production systems and received ball bearings from occupied and neutral countries, especially Sweden. Although it certainly hurt the German war effort, strategic bombing failed to halt the rapid growth of German industrial production during the final war years. What it did accomplish was to divert one-third of capacity to producing antiaircraft technologies, including fighters and 88-mm ammunition.[51] Needless to say, that benefit, which amounted to more than the entire German war production before Operation Barbarossa, was completely unanticipated by the strategic air forces of the interwar era. On the other hand, the opportunity costs consumed by the Allied bombing forces were also high. Let's not forget that the price of a single B-17 purchase was more than six Sherman tanks.

Incorporating the Internal Combustion Engine and Changing Basic Military Processes in Largely Correct Ways

The Soviet Red Army
No country transformed itself more profoundly than the Soviet Union during the interwar era. Stalin was dedicated to reversing Russia's eternal strategic weakness: its industrial backwardness relative to the West. While

---

[50] Rosen, 1991, pp. 155–70.

[51] Rosen, 1991, p. 169.

Peter the Great and Catherine the Great incorporated the early modern Western revolutions in science and warfare during the 18th century, Stalin confronted imperial Russia's limited capacity to import the Industrial Revolution. The brutal campaigns of agricultural collectivization and the heavy industrial focus of the initial Five-Year Plans were the famous consequences of Stalin's efforts to catch up and surpass the capitalist West. His embrace of technological progress, to the point of enlisting significant degrees of capitalist industrial expertise, also profoundly shaped the culture of the Soviet armed forces during the interwar era.

Key commanders of the Soviet Red Army were painfully aware of their backwardness, based on their humiliating performance against the Germans during World War I. They were also conscious that their ability to defeat the White Armies during the Russian Civil War had as much to do with the White Army's incompetence and divided commands as their own conduct. Yet for all of the Bolshevik infatuation with American mass production (i.e., Fordism and Taylorism) and German industrial R&D, the transformation of the Red Army from a poorly disciplined, lightly armed defensive force into a heavily industrialized and mechanized army by the late 1930s was astonishing.

Marshal Mikhail Tukhachevsky provided crucial leadership in reengineering the Red Army along mechanization lines. He secured the initially scarce financial and industrial resources at the expense of powerful domestic interests. Tukhachevsky also played a key role both in establishing an R&D infrastructure to produce weapons and in synthesizing revolutionary military doctrines for their use. Few military minds have enjoyed his simultaneous talents for political maneuvering, technical creativity, historical synthesis, strategic analysis, administrative skill, and military forecasting. He was the Bonaparte of military reengineering. The high degree of innovation that occurred within the Red Army with respect to the internal combustion engine during the first Five-Year Plan (1928–33) can be partially explained by reviewing Tukhachevsky's accomplishments up until his untimely death, at the age of 44, before a Russian People's Commissariat of Internal Affairs (NKVD) firing squad in 1937. Stalin could not tolerate the risk that he might be a Bonaparte in political realms as well.

An aristocratic junior officer in the Czarist army during World War I who nevertheless embraced Marxism, Tukhachevsky quickly advanced to senior Red Army ranks during the Russian Civil War. In that capacity he acquired firsthand experience in devising decisive military operations on a vast geographical scale and learned painful lessons about the demanding requirements in his unsuccessful offensive against Poland in 1920. Tukhachevsky's determination to overcome Russia's glaring military limitations was also revealed by the Red Army's unusual collaboration with the Reichswehr during the Weimar Republic. Based initially on mutual interest in countering the surprising military capability of the new Polish state, the collaboration succeeded for other reasons as well. The Germans, crippled by the harsh conditions of the Versailles Treaty, needed Soviet cover to test and develop tanks, aircraft, poison gas, and other forbidden military technologies, as well as to train officers. Likewise, the Soviet military leadership was eager to learn directly about German military doctrines, training methodologies, weapon systems, and officer education (especially for General Staff officers). Although fraught with distrust and disappointments, this collaboration gave the Red Army crucial insights into tank design, maintenance, training, and operations; it also provided significant degrees of pilot training and established virtually from scratch a chemical-warfare capability.[52] Such willingness to learn from foreign sources, even recent enemies, reflected the Red Army's willingness to synthesize the best innovations from eclectic international sources. Just as Peter the Great recognized the need for indigenous Russian scientific societies to support his Westernized military reforms, however, Tukhachevsky recognized the demand for indigenous Soviet R&D programs with respect to armor warfare in particular and mechanization in general. By the late 1920s, the Soviets were acquiring and evaluating Western designs and also synthesizing their best features with native design concepts.[53]

Perhaps Tukhachevsky's most formidable accomplishment was his successful lobbying of the Communist leadership to secure the funding and resources demanded by his ambitious mechanization plans. Not only did he work productively with Stalin and Voroshilov in spite of their distrust of professional military officers beyond the cavalry, he also

---

[52] Sally W. Stoecker, *Forging Stalin's Army: Marshal Tukhachevsky and the Politics of Military Innovation*, Boulder, Colo.: Westview Press, 1998, pp. 77–105.

[53] Stoecker, 1998, p. 116.

succeeded in outmaneuvering domestic interests in securing a sizeable portion of the first Five-Year Plan's budget for military mechanization. Given the low level of Russian industrialization in the late 1920s, where its per-capita industrialization level was the lowest in Europe (and its absolute level was lower than France's), this was quite an achievement. Part of Tukhachevsky's success with lobbying on behalf of the Red Army rested on his ability to leverage his arguments with Marxist philosophy, especially from Friedrich Engels. It also depended on his talent at maneuvering between the contradictory Stalinist extremes of technological progress and political conformity.[54] His scholarly sophistication went far beyond the confines of Marx, Engels, and Lenin, however.

Tukhachevsky was an avid student of military history, especially the works of Delbruck. As demonstrated by his monumental *Future War* (1928), he studied intensely the seemingly contradictory experiences of World War I and the Russian Civil War. Tukhachevsky concluded, unlike many cavalry commanders fixed on the Civil War, that both the Russian and German defeat in the Great War demanded serious strategic analysis. The key Russian weakness rested on a weak and poorly mobilized industrial infrastructure, especially when compared to France. Germany's classic limitation was in organizing its forces around a single strategy of decisive mobile warfare while ignoring the demands for long-term attritional warfare. This unusual willingness to transcend the myopia of his own army's experience in the war furnished Tukhachevsky with two fundamental transformation goals: to orient Soviet industrialization towards fulfilling the R&D and production demands of lengthy attritional warfare, and to furnish the Red Army with the internal-combustion technologies and doctrines to practice both strategies of attrition and annihilation. To support the development of innovative weapons systems, he set up the famous Gas Dynamics Laboratory to develop that other category of modern internal combustion: the rocket. The laboratory initiated the research for Katyusha rockets of World War II fame, as well as numerous bombs, torpedoes, and rocket-assisted takeoff devices for aircraft.[55] Korolov began his famous

---

[54] Stoecker, 1998, p. 142.

[55] Stoecker, 1998, p. 156.

career designing strategic and space missiles there. Tukhachevsky also supported the centralization of tank design and development laboratories that began in 1929.

Tukhachevsky's most influential accomplishment proved to be his leading role in developing Deep Operation theory, a sophisticated response to the promise of armored warfare. Essentially, the theory relied on the substantial military writings of the 1920s by such theorists as Triandafillov, Varfolomeev, Drasiln'nikov, Belitskii, and Tukhachevsky himself, as well as the broader military debates associated with Frunze and Svechin.[56] Deep Operation theory not only elaborated how to initially break enemy defenses, but also argued for the necessity of conducting local encircling operations to destroy frontline troops, coupled with raids deep into enemy territory, to eliminate supply depots, command posts, logistical networks, and lines of retreat. The central idea was to rupture enemy forces by simultaneously attacking deep strategic, intermediate logistical, and immediate combat targets. A key element was the maintenance of strategic reserves that could be thrust into emerging ruptures to achieve the necessary breakthrough. Tukhachevsky specified how the initial assault could be conducted with tanks, infantry, and artillery, along with additional mobile artillery units to consolidate initial breakthroughs. Following the formation of local encirclements to neutralize the defensive lines, the assault would conclude with the deployment of tanks, cavalry, and motorized infantry. To take full advantage of the penetration, air-assault units and paratroopers would aid the deep pursuits of the cavalry and armor into enemy territory.[57] The supplementary use of air-assault troops and paratroopers in such combined-arms operations was among Tukhachevsky's most original contributions to such mechanized-warfare doctrine.

Perhaps the most profound aspect of Deep Operation theory rested on its compatibility with a holistic "systems" approach to warfare, as opposed to the linear "mechanistic" perspective of the 19th century that dominated the combat of World War I. The former focused on maximizing the disorder of the enemy's military system, including logis-

---

[56] Jacob W. Kipp, 2000, pp. 126–38.

[57] Messenger, 1976, p. 86.

tics, command and control, transportation, intelligence networks, and frontline combat units. The latter, as articulated most prominently by Clausewitz, was oriented towards the destruction of the mass of enemy combat troops. Shimon Naveh argued, in fact, that Deep Operation theory was so sophisticated with its implicit system awareness that it appears compatible with the theoretical framework articulated by Bertalanffy in his *General Systems Theory*.[58] This includes such abstractions as open system, aim, non-linearity, cognitive tension, entropy or disruption, momentum, and synergy. Equally provocative is Naveh's assertion that the development of such theoretical sophistication did not come in direct response to Soviet mechanization efforts: its essential elements were already established by 1928. Such theory instead helped guide the remarkably successful armored warfare development of the Red Army when it occurred during the 1930s.[59] The highlights of this campaign included (1) synthesizing both foreign and domestic designs to furnish advance tank designs, (2) establishing mass-production facilities for their construction, and (3) organizing independent tank divisions for strategic action by the early 1930s. The Germans, by contrast, established their first panzer division only in 1935. Not surprisingly, many senior Soviet officers vigorously opposed such an open embrace of armored warfare, including many cavalry and infantry commanders who feared their traditional primacy would be undermined.[60] Nevertheless, the broad military and political acceptance of the Deep Operation theory was manifest by the mid-1930s. The Red Army's 1936 field regulations represented its fullest expression, where Tukhachevsky himself wrote a number of the chapters.

The ability of the Red Army to establish the doctrinal groundwork for the decisive armored warfare operations of the Great Patriotic War

---

[58] Ludwig von Bertalanffy, *General Systems Theory: Foundations, Development, Applications*, New York: Braziller, 1968.

[59] Shimon Naveh, *In Pursuit of Military Excellence: The Evolution of Operational Theory*, London: Frank Cass, 1997, pp. 179–80.

[60] Condoleezza Rice, "The Making of Soviet Strategy," in Peter Paret, ed., *Makers of Modern Strategy from Machiavelli to the Nuclear Age*, Princeton, N.J.: Princeton University Press, 1986, p. 666.

depended not only on theoretical constructions but also on the empirical observations of immediate military engagements. The Soviets practiced their first armored operation against the Kuomindang Army in 1929, following their seizure of the Chinese Eastern Railway. This furnished an early opportunity to test such light-tank prototypes as the T-26 (based on the Vickers-Armstrong 6-ton tank) and the BT (based on the Christie M1928 convertible tank).[61] A subsequent operation along the Sungari River tested air-ground assault landings and taught valuable lessons involving both naval and army artillery support, unifying the command of combined-arms operations and close-air support. Other operations further demonstrated the value of using tanks and aircraft together in encircling actions.[62] It was the conflicts against the Japanese in the late 1930s, however, that permitted full-scale tests of the Deep Operation theory. The frontal assaults against Japanese troops at Lake Khasan in 1938 confirmed a host of tactical ideas, including (1) the weakness of isolated air assaults on entrenched troops, (2) the dependence of infantry and tank units on artillery support, (3) the need for combined-arms operations in seizing prepared defenses, (4) the importance of using terrain features to minimize the exposure of tanks, and (5) the vulnerability of tanks to antitank guns when operating without infantry support.[63] Finally, it was Marshal Zhukov's ability to repulse the Japanese invasion of Outer Mongolia that first demonstrated Tukhachevsky's theories of operational shock with mechanized units. Not only did Zhukov cut the Japanese off from their lines of communication, following an extended campaign of deception, he also inflicted over 40,000 casualties for a price of 10,000 Soviet troops.

Unfortunately for the Soviet Union, such demonstrations failed to convince Stalin of the validity of Deep Operation theory. He suspected it was primarily a cover behind which Tukhachevsky could organize a coup; he therefore had the doctrine suppressed during the Red Army's purge of 1937–38. General Pavlov, after serving in the Spanish Civil War, thus persuaded Stalin that independent armor action was

---

[61] Stoecker, 1998, p. 67.

[62] Stoecker, 1998, p. 69.

[63] Messenger, 1976, p. 121.

doomed by new antitank weaponry. The only demonstrable utility of armor action, he argued, lay in close infantry support.[64] Consequently, Stalin ordered the breakup of the large tank divisions in 1939, only to reverse the order hastily in June 1940 following the fall of France. The chaotic re-re-reengineering during the Red Army's rapid expansion, the liquidation of the senior mechanization officers associated with Tukhachevsky, and Stalin's misreading of the strategic tea leaves set the stage for the Soviets' disastrous combat performances against the Finns in the winter of 1940 and the Germans in the summer of 1941. Yet the Soviet's ability to recover from its enormous initial losses and to learn how to systematically rupture the German defensive lines by the spring of 1943 rested heavily on the prewar Deep Operation theory as well as its formidable tank design and production facilities. Tukhachevsky and his armored warfare colleagues might have been eliminated before the war, but their ultimate influence on their younger replacements during World War II was unmistakable when Deep Operation theory was officially revived. Their work was also noted beyond the Soviet Union. After all, Hitler supposedly confessed to Guderian in 1944 that, had he been capable of believing Guderian's flattering comments about Soviet armored-warfare capabilities in *Achtung Panzer!* (1937), he would never have authorized Operation Barbarossa.[65]

The German Wehrmacht

The German army, or the Reichswehr, initially faced the most severe constraints of any interwar military organization. Because of the Versailles Treaty, it was reduced to 100,000 men and prohibited from using virtually all modern weapons systems, including airplanes, tanks, and poison gas. Its most strategic asset, the General Staff Corps, was also abolished. The victorious allies of the Great War were determined to

---

[64] John Erickson, *The Soviet High Command: A Military-Political History*, Boulder, Colo.: Westview Press, 1984, p. 537.

[65] Guderian, 1957, pp. 151–54. Guderian concluded the following, after claiming the Russians had the world's strongest army with 10,000 tanks: "The time has passed when the Russians had no instinct for technology; we will have to reckon on the Russians being able to master and build their own machines, and with the fact that such a transformation in the Russians' fundamental mentality confronts us with the Eastern Question in a form more serious than ever before in history."

eliminate Germany's ability to wage foreign wars of aggression and to reduce its powerful military institutions to little more than internal security forces. The effort was a profound failure. The humiliating defeat of World War I, coupled with the drastic restrictions of the Versailles Treaty, helped stimulate undoubtedly the most celebrated military reengineering programs in history (especially from an American perspective).[66]

To understand the strengths and limitations of this bold reengineering effort, one must first recognize the Reichswehr's efforts to retain only the best features of the Second Reich's Imperial Army. Thanks to some quick thinking, Ludendorff's successor and future War Minister, General Wilhelm Goerning, convinced the Kaiser to abdicate. This liberated the army from the decentralization it endured in the imperial administration. Instead of answering to both the local kingdoms and the Prussian Kaiser, it could then be centralized under the military leadership of the commander in chief.[67] The Second Reich had also forced the army to submit to the often conflicting leadership of both the General Staff and the War Ministry. The former was responsible for doctrine, training, strategy and grand tactics, and field commands; the latter was responsible for procurement and funding.[68] Following the revolutionary chaos of the early Weimar Republic, the new Chief of the General Staff, Hans von Seeckt, successfully reorganized these two bodies as the Truppenamt and Waffenamt, respectively, and kept them firmly under his control.

If the defeat in World War I managed to eliminate the inefficient organizational legacy of the Imperial Army, the conditions of the Versailles Treaty failed to eradicate its powerful cultural foundations.

---

[66] For an example of the most recent praise of the Wehrmacht's transformation efforts, see James S. Corum, "A Comprehensive Approach to Change," in Harold Winton and David Mets, eds., *The Challenge of Change: Military Institutions and New Realities, 1918–1941*, Lincoln and London: University of Nebraska Press, 2000. Corum concludes, "Judging by its operational competence the German army's program of reform during the interwar period has to count as one of the most successful examples of military reform at the tactical and operational levels of war" (66–67).

[67] Wilhelm Deist, "The Road to Ideological War: Germany, 1918–1945," in W. Murray, M. Knox, and A. Bernstein, eds., *The Making of Strategy: Rulers, States, and War*, Cambridge: Cambridge University Press, 1994, pp. 354–55.

[68] Corum, 2000, p. 43.

In fact, it helped intensify these foundations. The old Prussian military tradition represented a synthesis of the disciplined and ruthlessly drilled armies of Frederick Wilhelm II and Frederick the Great and the Enlightenment ideals of *Bildung*, strategic reasoning, scientific objectivity, and technical progress embodied by the General Staff system. This system for outthinking Napoléon was the brainchild of Scharnhorst, who established it in the aftermath of Prussia's debilitating defeat by Napoleon at Jena-Auerstaedt in 1806.[69] Prussia's Chief of the General Staff during the Wars of Unification (1864–71), Helmuth von Moltke, leveraged these conceptual foundations to strengthen the General Staff dramatically. It became capable of rapidly testing, optimizing and incorporating the new technologies of the Second Industrial Revolution, especially railroads, mass-produced steel, and telegraphs, within the context of Bismarck's grand strategy. To maintain this organization, in spite of its prohibition by the Treaty of Versailles, Seeckt replaced front-line officers with highly educated General Staff officers in the coveted officer positions of the Reichswehr. He also camouflaged their proscribed staff and research work under the Truppenamt. This concentration of elite staff officers furnished an essential prerequisite for Seeckt's ambition to transform the Reichswehr into a highly professional organization, capable of engaging in a continuous development of modern weaponry and tactics with an emphasis on offensive mobile warfare.

As a senior staff general in the eastern fronts of the Great War, Seeckt witnessed what well-trained and relatively mobile German forces could do to the massive, yet poorly coordinated armies of Czarist Russia. The success of the motorized British infantry, as well as that of the horse cavalry forces against the Ottoman armies he later helped direct, must have left a deep impression. Given the severe treaty constraints, Seeckt concluded that only a highly professional force (however small) that specialized in mobile, if not motorized, warfare, could meet the defense needs of the Weimar Republic. In effect, much of his effort as commander in chief from 1920 to 1926 lay both in eradicating the trench-warfare mentality that many officers acquired and in developing effective

---

[69] Charles White, *The Enlightened Soldier: Scharnhorst and the Militärische Gesellschaft in Berlin, 1801–1805*, New York: Praeger, 1989.

doctrines for modern mobile warfare based on intensive historical, technical, and experimental studies. Seeckt started by authorizing perhaps the most intensive historical study ever conducted of World War I, one that involved hundreds of officers. Here, he concluded that the German army's key weaknesses included its logistical failure to sustain the initial offensive into France in 1914 and to support the breakthroughs achieved by the storm troopers during the final offensive in 1918. In other words, Seeckt's study directly confronted the uncoordinated logistical planning surrounding the Schlieffen Plan and acknowledged how much the German General Staff had arrogantly retreated from deeper operational thought before the Great War. For example, the Staff had stockpiled only six month's worth of munitions, which would have led to a military collapse by mid-1915 had I. G. Farben not rescued them with its innovative new process for synthesizing nitrates.

Seeckt's style of leadership, with all its hostility to the trench-warfare tactics of the Western Front, contrasted sharply to the French fixation on Methodical Warfare. In spite of his centralized power, Seeckt *heightened* the General Staff's rigorous intellectual atmosphere throughout the German army. Critical, skeptical, and analytical attitudes superseded dogmatic conformity. As a consequence, dissent within the officer ranks was tolerated and, when effectively presented and backed up, seriously considered. After all, Seeckt's ideals of mobile offensive warfare and sophisticated combined-arms tactics were not only based on his experience from World War I; they also evolved from the traditional General Staff methodologies of historical and technical studies, war gaming, experimental testing in full-scale maneuvers, and comparative analyses of international developments. No army in the 1920s invested as much in field exercises as the Germans did under Seeckt. Military investments extended to such prohibited technologies as tanks and airplanes, which were incorporated into experimental maneuvers through the use of wooden models, balloons, and civilian vehicles. Furthermore, no army subjected the results to such careful scrutiny.

Like his American counterparts, Seeckt was also committed to establishing a force structure that could be efficiently expanded in the event of a national emergency or a lifting of the Versailles Treaty. Nevertheless, he went much further. Seeckt instigated extremely high performance standards for the officer corps, allowing officers to command at levels two to three higher than their current rank and to serve in different units. Infantry officers, for instance, were routinely trained to serve as artillery officers, while cavalry officers were expected to double as machine-gun commanders. It is within this spirit that the motorized-transport troops, responsible for maintaining and driving the supply vehicles, were also expected to develop motorized-combat tactics. Such expectations were essential for effective combined-arms tactics. The training of new officers subsequently expanded into a four-year program that coupled demanding academic examinations with intensive combat leadership training to promote the self-initiative of frontline commanders—an essential prerequisite for mobile warfare. The competitive pressures coming from the large number of demobilized officers eager to resume their service helped permit such strict demands.

Seeckt also emphasized the training and education of the enlisted ranks. Virtually all privates, for example, were trained to serve as non-commissioned officers (NCOs) when the anticipated expansion finally arrived. One can argue that Seeckt's success lay not in advocating *Bewegungskrieg,* or mobile warfare, and setting the doctrinal foundations for the Blitzkrieg of World War II. Rather, his true achievements lay in strengthening the rich Prussian military tradition of objective historical study; in fostering a stimulating intellectual environment that promoted flexible, tolerant, and ultimately constructive doctrinal debates; and, finally, in advancing extensive training and experimental exercises.[70] By updating such processes, the outright rejection of the French Methodical Battle by the mid-1920s and the creation of the panzer divisions by the mid-1930s proved to be relatively smooth evolutions. As early as 1926, when Seeckt resigned after committing some trivial yet offensive political blunders, the essential foundations for effective mechanized warfare were in place. These included (1) the relative decentralization of combat command structures to ensure effective initiative of frontline leadership; (2) the rejection of a continuous World War I–style front; (3) the focus on attacking the *Schwerpunkt,*

---

[70] James S. Corum, *The Roots of Blitzkrieg: Hans von Seeckt and the German Military Reform,* Lawrence: University of Kansas Press, 1992, p. xvi.

or center of gravity, of enemy forces; (4) the maintenance of close air support; and (5) the primacy of retaining offensive momentum even when lacking secured flanks.[71]

It was then Heinz Guderian who designed and constructed the panzer divisions during the mid-1930s.[72] Here, he encountered much opposition to his concept of concentrating the scarce mechanized resources of the divisions. Many infantry and artillery officers countered that these resources should be distributed throughout the army in light of Germany's limited industrial capacity and material resources.[73] In spite of such resistance, Guderian succeeded with reengineering on a tactical level, unlike his counterparts in other nations. Much of this success can be attributed to the first-rate conceptual, organizational, and operational conditions that Seeckt had solidified. Guderian above all valued Seeckt's established testing and experimental methodologies, which included realistic "red teaming." Volckheim and other early armored-warfare students in Germany conducted extensive doctrinal studies involving critical yet thorough studies of foreign armored warfare developments. Their work did not preclude Guderian from modifying some of his theoretical ideas about a panzer division's components when subjected to actual field tests. The exercises with dummy tanks in 1933 convinced him of the need for fully motorized support troops. Yet he did not shift the balance to having more engineering and infantry support troops and fewer tanks until after the Treaty of Versailles was lifted in 1935. Only then was it permissible to test a full-scale experimental panzer division. Likewise, the maneuvers of 1937 revealed the poor coordination of the repair and refueling system, a problem that continued to plague Guderian during the invasion of Austria in 1938. The long distance his panzer division traveled from Würtzburg to Vienna also revealed numerous problems with mechanical reliability: between 30 and 70 percent of his tanks broke down. Such full-scale testing revealed

---

[71] Corum, 2000, p. 42.

[72] Despite the self-serving claims on this score by Guderian himself after the war (claims more recently articulated as an example of conventional organizational behavior), his success was hardly the drama of a lone hero fighting other intransigent officers and aided only by the intervention of Hitler.

[73] Deighton, 1979, p. 122.

the efficacy of first-rate wireless and optical instruments, as well as the need for armored command vehicles to ensure effective leadership from the front lines. Such testing further strengthened Guderian's conviction in the face of armored warfare skeptics.[74] By 1938, his opponents were momentarily empowered by the increasing strength of French and Czech heavy fortifications, the tank's marginal performance in Spain, and the German infantry's resistance to relying exclusively on horse-drawn wagons. Far more serious, however, were the leading Wehrmacht commanders who started addressing Nazi Germany's industrial inability to match the material needs of the rapidly expanding Wehrmacht. Their confrontation with Hitler culminated with his orders to plan for an invasion of Czechoslovakia.

The Soviet Union did not have a monopoly on officers who were capable of sophisticated operational thinking. During the early years of the Third Reich, a group of senior officers led by Ludwig Beck, Chief of the General Staff, was determined to preserve the General Staff's control of strategic and operational planning. The group's mission was to ensure that the Wehrmacht would remain grounded in economic and industrial reality in spite of the growing pressures of Nazi ideology. This reality was subsequently manifested in Beck's *Truppenführung HD-30*—the high point in operational theory for the Wehrmacht. Like Tukhachevsky, Beck advocated strategic and operational planning based on universal principles grounded in history, rather than ad hoc planning based on particular developments.[75] Far from being hostile to armored warfare, as Guderian maintained, Beck argued instead that sound military operations must depend on combined-arms actions, not on any particular weapon system. Likewise, he was painfully aware of how demanding such actions were on German industry. He also repudiated Schlieffen's 19th-century *Kesselschlacht* ideal of winning wars in one offensive campaign of annihilation. Rather, he emphasized the need for successive operations that were balanced for both offensive and defensive actions. Beck's broad strategic and operational

---

[74] However egocentric, Guderian's autobiography, *Panzer Leader* (1957), provides an excellent overview of at least the technical struggles he faced in developing the panzer division.

[75] Naveh, 1997, p. 117. I rely on Naveh's work for the following perspective on Beck as well.

awareness naturally conflicted with the "technocratic" elements of the Wehrmacht, as represented by Guderian, if not Rommel, who focused exclusively on technological development and tactical efficiency. Given the growing tension facing Beck and other senior staff officers who recognized the widening gulf between Hitler's growing military ambitions and the economic realities of German industry, such a technical or tactical focus became increasingly common for ambitious officers who were willing to suppress any operational insight to gain Hitler's favor. To drive the point home, Beck was forced to resign by 1938: he had confronted Hitler about the profound irresponsibility of risking a world war that an invasion of Czechoslovakia would provoke, given Germany's inadequate logistical and industrial resources.

Unlike the Russians and the Americans, whose leadership devoted considerable attention to the strategic question of industrial mobilization, the Wehrmacht was hamstrung by Nazi internal policies. Hitler was especially sensitive to German public opinion of the material standard of living; the willingness of starving Germans to overthrow the Second Reich in 1918 had left a dark impression on him. He was also pressured by labor and business interests who feared losing market shares in the civilian economy because of heavy military contracts.[76] Hence, any mobilization effort that would undermine the Germans' access to consumer goods was prohibited well into World War II. Likewise, there was never an optimized distribution of the scarce metal workers between active military service and strategic industrial production. Guderian, in fact, failed to suppress his frustration with being unable to procure sufficient numbers of medium-weight Panzer III and IV tanks during the late 1930s; instead, he had to rely extensively on the tough little Czech tanks during the initial campaigns of World War II.

The formal suppression of operational considerations in the Wehrmacht was executed by Hitler's sacking of not only Beck but also the War Minister, General Werner von Blomberg, and Commander in

---

[76] Bernard R. Kroener, "Squaring the Circle: Blitzkrieg Strategy and Manpower Shortage, 1939–1942," in Wilhelm Deist, ed., *The German Military in the Age of Total War*, Dover, England: Berg Publishers, 1985, pp. 284–85.

Chief, Werner Freiherr von Fritsch, in 1938. This opened the flood-gates for an ever-frantic focus on tactical effectiveness. This was evinced by a growing acceptance to combine mechanized forces with the old 19th-century *Kesselschlacht* ideal to achieve an encirclement that could maximize the destruction of frontline enemy troops.[77] This is what would become known in World War II as *Blitzkrieg,* essentially a tactical technique without theoretical grounding that was scaled up to guide the conduct of an entire army. Against poorly equipped and even more poorly commanded troops such as the Poles, Norwegians, or Yugoslavs, the tactical opportunism of the Blitzkrieg worked wonders. On the other hand, against more formidable forces such as the British and Americans in North Africa or the Soviets in their motherland, this technique fell apart. Ironically enough, Blitzkrieg's greatest claim to fame was in the Western campaign of 1940. Yet, as Naveh has argued, this was not a Blitzkrieg campaign at all, but rather a classic example of sophisticated operational planning, thanks to the capable leadership of Erich von Manstein. Von Manstein had commanded the General Staff's operations division and had served under Beck as Deputy Chief of Staff.[78] Given the total of strategic direction from Hitler, he sought to divide the Allied armies and defeat them separately. That the operation emerged as an encirclement of the Allied forces in Belgium came as a considerable surprise, as evidenced by the considerable trepidation and confusion the German command experience following the break-through at Sedan.

The famed German Blitzkrieg, in short, was largely an improvised affair that succeeded against tactically inferior forces that exercised little operational planning. When subjected to the attrition and vast expanses of the Eastern Front or North African desert, all the tactical brilliance of Guderian, Rommel, and other disciples of Seeckt could not compensate for a fundamental lack of strategic planning and coordination. It is here that the Soviet Union's accomplishment stands in stark contrast. The Red Army never had any illusion that war with Germany would not be a brutal, costly, and lengthy affair. However weak their

---

[77] Naveh, 1997, p. 124.

[78] Naveh, 1997, p. 126.

command structure, training procedures, officer experience, and troop morale were in the spring of 1941, the Soviets were nevertheless able to offset these shortcomings with their powerful military-industrial coordination and their willingness to relearn their Deep Operations theory. The Germans too sought to revive their operational cognition when the harsh reality of invading the Soviet Union became unmistakable, but it proved to be too little too late. Of course, this is to not to say that the German reengineering effort of the interwar era was ultimately a failure. Much of what the Reichswehr and Wehrmacht accomplished during the interwar era represents model military reengineering from both tactical and operational perspectives. Hitler's corrosive influence on the Wehrmacht, especially its opportunistic officers, ultimately inflicted far greater damage to such reengineering accomplishments than Stalin's purge of the Red Army. However destructive the prewar execution of thousands of senior officers proved to be from 1941 to 1942, the German dictator could not irrevocably reverse the interwar reengineering campaigns involving Soviet industry, armored warfare, and operational planning.

The U.S. Marine Corps

Perhaps the U.S. Marine Corps drummed up the most effective military reengineering program of the interwar era. Unlike the German panzer divisions, whose tactical success rested both on a rich tradition of military excellence and on steady financial, technical, and political support, the Marine Corps was routinely dismissed by jealous competitors as a second-rate military organization. It was seen by many of its critics as fit primarily for providing guard duty and suppressing the occasional minor conflicts within the United States's sphere of influence. Even following the Marines' outstanding combat service on the Western Front in World War I, leading naval commanders such as Admiral William Sims found it hard to imagine that individual Marines were capable of conducting heavy military operations and that officers were intelligent enough to lead large units of men. Such disdain was reflected by the Marine Corps's total dependence on the Navy for its financial resources, the impossibility of letting a senior Marine officer command significant naval resources, and the encouragement of only the worst Naval Academy graduates to accept Marine Corps commissions. After all, it was argued, the Marines contributed only marginally to the Navy's primary mission of engaging and destroying large surface fleets.[79] All of this was to change in the years ahead.

It is within this context that the leading officers of the Marine Corps began to take seriously the implications of both the failed British campaign at Gallipoli and the vast expansion of Japanese territory in the central Pacific. The latter included the Marshall and Caroline Islands, which stretched ominously towards Hawaii. General Lejeune had been struggling since before World War I to define a unique Marine Corps combat mission. To support a major naval campaign, he had postulated the utility of being able to seize and defend advanced bases.[80] Yet given the routine conclusion that Gallipoli "proved" it was impossible to conduct an amphibious assault against a fortified enemy resistance, it was assumed that the seizing phase of such an operation would only work with unoccupied beaches. Unfortunately, numerous small islands of the central Pacific furnished the Japanese with bases that flanked the main naval approaches to their home islands; as such, the local garrison could easily detect and resist any amphibious assault. An American naval offensive against Japan only had a chance if some means existed to do the impossible; that is, to conduct an amphibious assault against a prepared enemy resistance would require a miracle.

Major Earl H. Ellis was a highly decorated Marine Corps staff officer who served with distinction in the final campaigns of World War I. He not only grasped the strategic dilemma of the central Pacific in the early 1920s, he also applied his brilliant military mind to resolving the intractable dilemma of amphibious assault. With the strong support of General Lejeune, who gradually recognized this problem as the unique combat mission essential for the Marine Corps's longevity, Ellis completed in 1921 his famous secret report entitled *Advanced Base Operations in Micronesia*. He described

---

[79] John P. Campbell, "Marines, Aviators and the Battleship Mentality, 1923–33," in Merrill L. Bartlett, ed., *Assault from the Sea: Essays on the History of Amphibious Warfare*, Annapolis, Md.: Naval Institute Press, 1983, p. 171. See also Holland M. Smith and Percy Finch, *Coral and Brass*, Washington, D.C.: Zenger Publishing, 1979, pp. 47–50.

[80] Robert Debs Heinl, Jr., *Soldiers of the Sea: The United States Marine Corps, 1775–1962*, Annapolis, Md.: U.S. Naval Institute, 1962, p. 253.

in detail the likely naval conflict with Japan, starting with their onslaught across the Pacific, followed by an American counterattack straight through the Marshalls and the Carolines.[81] His broad strategic conceptions were backed up with detailed tactical studies of amphibious assault—not surprising given his successful plans for attacking the heavily fortified Blanc Mont Ridge in 1918. He recommended using the cover of darkness to assemble the boats for the assault, but only to release them in the early morning hours: nighttime assaults were simply too complicated to coordinate in the dark. For the actual assault to succeed, a complex joint and combined-arms operation would be required. Air bombing, strafing, and naval firepower would commence the attack, while assault troops would be assisted on land by support personnel serving in light artillery, wireless communication, naval artillery spotting, combat engineering, and logistics units.[82] Taking a cue from the storm-trooper tactics on the final German offensive of 1918, the essential element would be a heavy, fast-moving, yet unrelenting offensive that relied on close coordination, rigorous training, and innovative weaponry.

Advanced Base Operations would serve, after Ellis's death from alcoholism while spying the Japanese central Pacific islands in 1923, as the blueprint for the Marine Corps's reengineering effort. Rarely in military history has the reengineering of a new military process been based on such accurate doctrine.

Developing Ellis's amphibious assault doctrine proved to be an exceedingly difficult task for the Marine Corps. In addition to limited funding, the Marines faced the distraction of expeditionary campaigns in China and Nicaragua, naval bureaucratic intransigence, increasingly limited funding, Army-absorption ambitions, and widespread skepticism. As inspiring as Ellis's studies were to such ambitious Marine officers as Holland "Howlin' Mad" Smith, John Russell, and John Lejeune, the Navy remained largely unconvinced. Too many issues remained, as top Navy brass never tired to explain in the 1920s. No motorized assault boat existed or could be easily conceived of that could be conveniently

---

[81] John J. Reber, "Pete Ellis: Amphibious Warfare Prophet," in Merrill L. Bartlett, ed., *Assault from the Sea: Essays on the History of Amphibious Warfare*, Annapolis, Md.: Naval Institute Press, 1983, p. 158.

[82] Reber, 1983, p. 158.

assembled, loaded with Marines, launched quickly through coral and heavy surf to deliver their human cargo safely to the beachhead, and conveniently returned to the ship. Delivering the necessary fire support from battleships was likewise deemed impossible. Not only did it conflict with Nelson's traditional maxim about the folly of using ships to attack forts, it was thought to be technically impossible to maneuver rapidly through the waters (to avoid defensive ground fire) while delivering accurate fire aim. From a broader perspective, the new Marine infatuation with amphibious assault irked the leading Navy commanders with its unmistakable implication: the Marines would emerge as the primary offensive force, whereas the Navy would be reduced to furnishing only the supportive transport, artillery, air, and logistic services.

The Marines' ultimate success in amphibious warfare during World War II came only after almost 20 years of painstaking frustrations involving historical study, experimental testing—both tactically and technically—and doctrinal development. Fortunately, they had an excellent role model in the potential Japanese enemy, whose mastery of amphibious warfare operations was effective, especially against China.[83] Nevertheless, it was the negative example of Gallipoli that furnished the primary historical case study that occupied so much of the attention of the Marine Corps School (MCS). Marines began to reorient their studies towards amphibious warfare in 1926 and analyzed every conceivable aspect of that campaign with a mania for detail, if not objectivity, like that of a German General Staff. The breadth of the project is revealed by the basic components of the project, which included studies of high-level leadership failures, breakdowns in command hierarchies, a lack of specialized equipment and material, poor ship-to-shore communications, ineffectual naval bombardments, and poorly organized logistical support.[84] These basic shortcomings, in turn, represented doctrinal challenges that the MCS was intent on solving.

By 1929, the doctrinal studies of the MCS at Quantico began to furnish concrete recommendations for the organization of command

---

[83] Allan R. Millett, "Assault from the Sea: The Development of Amphibious Warfare Between the Wars: The American, British, and Japanese Experiences," in William Murray and Allan Millet, eds., *Military Innovation in the Interwar Period*, Cambridge: Cambridge University Press, 1996, pp. 64–70.

relations between naval and land forces, gunfire and air support, and the embarkation and loading of assault craft in combat, along with the desirable technical characteristics of such craft. Its progress was aided by the chaotic early experiments in amphibious warfare conducted by the Marines at Culebra (1924–25). In addition to digesting the problematic performance of the British "beetle boat" used at Gallipoli, as well as that of Christie's amphibious tank, the U.S. Marines were overwhelmed by the challenges of delivering sufficient forces in the initial attack wave and maintaining sufficient ship-to-shore coordination.[85] In spite of such distractions as expeditions to China and Nicaragua, not to mention Herbert Hoover's schemes to have them absorbed by the U.S. Army, the Marines did make progress: in 1933, the Navy authorized the first unit dedicated to amphibious assault, the Fleet Marine Force (FMF). The following year, the MCS furnished this new force with its official doctrine, *The Tentative Manual for Joint Operations*. Although acknowledging ongoing limitations, this doctrine emphasized the essential role of heavy naval fire support, close air support, unity of command, rapid delivery of field artillery and tanks, restriction of equipment to fit the cargo holds, arming of assault craft, and careful placement of loads that reflected the order of their delivery to the beachhead. Proving the validity of the doctrine's recommendations, as well as refining the strengths and correcting the weaknesses of them, became the task of the annual fleet landing exercises (FLEX) conducted from 1935 to 1939. These proved essential in practicing full-scale assaults and testing state-of-the-art radio communications equipment, dive-bombing attacks, and naval fire-support tactics using high-explosive artillery shells. Especially critical was the Navy's training and deployment of new fire-support liaison officers with Marine forces. By 1940, the Navy authorized a separate Base-Defense Force, designed for rapid defensive deployment to threatened Pacific bases to help maintain the FMF's focus on amphibious offensive action.[86]

---

[84] Robert D. Heinl, Jr., "The U.S. Marine Corps: Author of Modern Amphibious Warfare," in Merrill L. Bartlett, ed., *Assault from the Sea: Essays on the History of Amphibious Warfare*, Annapolis, Md.: Naval Institute Press, 1983, p. 187.

[85] Kenneth J. Clifford, *Amphibious Warfare Development in Britannia and America from 1920–1940*, Laurens: Edgewood, 1983, p. 32.

Such reengineering progress in the 1930s, however, was not matched by the procurement of suitable assault craft—the central technological prerequisite for any amphibious assault operation.

In 1933, the Navy authorized the formation of the Marine Corps Equipment Board to oversee the procurement of the specialized equipment required by the FMF. During the early FLEX experiments, the Equipment Board continued testing a wide range of assault boats. By 1938, it completely rejected the use of the Atlantic fishing-style boats. Their high bows made it difficult for Marines to disembark easily, and their exposed propellers and rudders hampered a rapid withdrawal. In addition, because of their heavy weight and curved sides, these boats proved difficult to lower, hoist, and store. The Navy's official design center remained unconvinced, however, and continued modifying its "Bureau Boats" along these problematic commercial lines. As late as 1941, the Marines still had to resist using heavier tank-lighter versions of these Navy-sponsored vessels: they were too massive to hoist from ships and remove from beaches, and too difficult to maneuver and maintain.

Fortunately, the Marines Corps discovered in 1937 the innovative boat conceptions of Andrew Higgins, whose vessels were originally designed for the shallow, vegetation-infested waters of the Mississippi delta.[87] The Marines conclusively demonstrated the utility of his innovations during the full-scale amphibious assault maneuvers at New River, North Carolina, in 1941 and 1942. Higgins imitated the Japanese there by placing a folding ramp in his boat's bow. Following a major bureaucratic struggle with the Bureau of Ships, Higgins finally supplied the authorized designs for the Landing Craft, Vehicle, Personnel, and Ramp (LCVP), as well as the Landing Craft, Medium (LCM), which served as a tank lighter. Just as infantry officers have shuddered at how they would have fought World War II without Garand's intrusion into the muddled interwar Ordnance Department with his product and tooling designs for the M-1 rifle, Marine Corps and Navy commanders have wondered how they would have fought the Pacific

---

[86] Heinl, 1983, p. 188.

[87] Jerry E. Strahan, *Andrew Jackson Higgins and the Boats That Won World War II*, Baton Rouge: Louisiana State University Press, 1994, p. 15.

campaign without Higgins's interference with the equally troubled Bureau of Boats. The adoption of Roebling's Landing Craft, Tracked (LCT), also known as the "alligator," represented a similar story of bureaucratic intransigence. Originally designed to maneuver through the Florida Everglades for rescue missions, it emerged as the ultimate amphibious vehicle, whose tracks propelled it on both land and sea.[88] Due to its lightweight aluminum design, the Marines initially assigned it to logistical support tasks. Only when facing the prospect of crossing the treacherous reefs of Tarawa were Roebling's alligators given their first of many combat assault roles.

The Marine Corps succeeded admirably at forging a doctrine specifically formulated for the actual battles of the Pacific. It also pursued an evolutionary training and procurement process to ensure the doctrine's practical realization. Such success, however, did not eliminate having to engage in sobering corrections in response to the formidable Japanese defenders of the central Pacific islands. This was especially the case after the Battle of Tarawa—the first full-scale amphibious assault on a fortified Japanese position. Insufficient naval fire support was a primary deficiency: far more rounds of heavy, armor-piercing shells were required to neutralize heavily fortified pillboxes and other reinforced-concrete structures. The corps also had to recognize the adverse effects of damp combat conditions on radio equipment. In turn, it identified the need for additional landing vehicle tanks (LVTs), flamethrowers, medium tanks, and field artillery. Equally perturbing, the logistical support proved to be poorly organized. These problems, however, did not invalidate the sound foundation of the Marine Corps's amphibious warfare doctrine.

The Marine Corps's and Navy's persistent analysis and correction process is a testament to their success with amphibious warfare. They demonstrated this with the assault on Kwajalein in the Marshalls and with the high standards of the naval fire-support school at Kahoolawee. On the other hand, the terrible Marine casualties that Japanese light-artillery fire inflicted at Saipan brought home another tragic lesson: the need to subject all possible artillery sites to a heavy preliminary bom-

---

[88] Clifford, 1983, p. 118.

bardment, whether or not guns were actually spotted.[89] This lesson was manifest at Iwo Jima, where naval gunners and pilots shifted from general saturation bombardment to a systematic sector-by-sector gunnery that often zeroed in on individual gun placements. The Marines nevertheless endured a bloody struggle in routing out the most formidable fortification network of the Pacific War. More Marines were lost in a few weeks at Iwo Jima than in the entire campaign for Guadalcanal:[90] the 20,000 Japanese entrenched at Iwo Jima inflicted more than 6,000 American deaths. As formidable as the Marine Corps's reengineering effort was—from transforming what was regarded as a support force into an invincible assault force that spearheaded the Pacific offensive (at least after 1942), the reality of modern entrenched firepower remained a horrifying force to confront.

---

[89] Donald M. Weller, "The Development of Naval Gunfire Support in World War II," in Merrill L. Bartlett, ed., *Assault from the Sea: Essays on the History of Amphibious Warfare*, Annapolis, Md.: Naval Institute Press, 1983, pp. 274–75.

[90] On the other hand, the U.S. Army suffered about as many casualties during the month-long Ardennes campaign as the Marine Corps suffered in the entire Pacific campaign: about 15,000 dead and 80,000 wounded. To the Army's credit, it faced 600,000 German troops spearheaded by their dreaded Panzer Corps, and it initially fought without air support.

CHAPTER THREE

Necessary Conditions for Military Reengineering

Observations

What then can we cull from the military reengineering efforts associated with mechanization during the interwar era? A number of observations are possible.

The tabula rasa is a myth. I can state, categorically, that in none of the interwar reengineerings did the military leaders start with a blank sheet of paper.[1] Although Tukhachevsky appears to have come close, his reengineering effort applied to only a relatively small section of the Red Army. As with the Wehrmacht, the vast majority of Russian troops continued to maneuver themselves tactically by marching. These armies never engaged in a sudden, radical transformation. Instead, they preferred to pursue evolutionary strategies accompanied by intensive study, debate, testing, and adjustment over lengthy periods of time.[2] However impressive the Wehrmacht was in organizing its panzer divisions in 1935 and subjecting them to combat by 1939, its success rested on

---

[1] Nor are examples evident in other periods. The possible exception might be the Japanese army and navy following the overthrow of the Shogun in the mid-19th century, thus launching their Westernizing Meiji Restoration Era.

[2] Some of these were akin to the "pragmatic reengineering" discussed in Paul K. Davis, *Planning Force Transformations: Learning from Both Successes and Failures*, Santa Monica, Calif.: RAND Corporation, unpublished, 2001; and Paul Bracken, *Reengineering and Information Technology: Relationships and Lessons Learned*, Santa Monica, Calif., RAND Corporation, unpublished manuscript. Others took longer and were more like the kind of process discussed briefly by Davis, but in more detail in Richard O. Hundley, *Past Revolutions, Future Transformations: What Can the History of Revolutions in Military Affairs Tell Us About Transforming the U.S. Military?* Santa Monica, Calif.: RAND Corporation, 1999.

many years of small-scale research, training, and observation during the Weimar Republic and early Third Reich.

Legacy systems are not jettisoned early on. A related broad conclusion is that military reengineering rarely involves the outright elimination of existing military processes or organizations. The "creative destruction" associated with Hammer and Champy's version of reengineering, not to mention Schumpeter's economic theories, was virtually nonexistent during the interwar era. Many military organizations experienced significant downsizing, but the reasons were domestic (except for Germany) and the downsizing was not seen as part of reengineering. On the contrary, traditional systems and processes were protected. The possible exception was the Reichswehr. When ordered to cut back its forces drastically after the Great War, it chose to preserve its core for what would be a transformed force.

A general rule in reengineering—one based on description, not prescription—suggests that innovations only augment traditional force structures. They do not reconstruct entire organizations abruptly. When successful, however, elite reengineered units can influence the traditional main force, but only in a gradualist, nondisruptive manner that may take a full generation to implement. Nonetheless, full implementation may require a calamity to make it a necessity.

As an aside, this rule appears to extend back to the late Middle Ages, when separate formations of firearm-wielding infantrymen were recruited and maintained directly by both Christian monarchs and Muslim sultans, as opposed to traditional feudal levies.

Even "good" reengineerings have rough beginnings. Another general lesson is the inevitable shortcomings of initial military reengineering efforts—even the successful ones. Despite the general success of the Marine Corps and the Wehrmacht with reengineering, their initial performance in heavy combat conditions left much to be desired in Tarawa and Poland, respectively. Numerous shortcomings emerged that required immediate training and process modifications.

Rapid military reengineering requires strong ground laying. It is also evident that reengineering cannot be rushed, as demonstrated by the experiences of France and the Soviet Union after the invasion of Poland. Clearly, rapid, large-scale reengineerings are extremely disruptive.

Another data point here is the U.S. Army Air Corps and its ground-based counterparts in the tank divisions, which began changing flawed processes once the war began but were not finished even late in the war. The Soviets *were* able to recover and rebuild more quickly—and began defeating German armies routinely by 1943; however, this was aided significantly by the sound basis laid in the 1930s by Tukhachevsky—and his close colleagues.

Communications matter greatly. Another observation is that communications technologies were powerful enablers of the mechanization-related transformations. The use of radar in the RAF air-defensive network used during the Battle of Britain is the most famous example. We might also remember, however, that Guderian received his initial combat experience in World War I as a signal officer and became proficient in radio-communication engineering. This background helped him appreciate the potential of independent armored units. Patton's insistence on increasing the power of the radios in his tanks (which led to a confrontation with the Signal Corps that was resolved at the highest levels) permitted the installation of long-range FM radios; this helped enable Patton's deep armored invasions into France and Germany. On the negative side, if Tukhachevsky had any weaknesses in his Deep Battle doctrine, it was his underestimation of the potential of radio communication. Soviet tanks had serious tactical limitations in the early phase of Operation Barbarossa because the Soviets had restricted radios only to the command tanks.

General Features of Successful Reengineering

The central issue remains one of identifying and articulating the fundamental independent variables that military leaders can control when seeking the challenge and opportunity of reengineering (or other forms of transformation). No simple formula is likely, since a great deal depends on situational details, such as how future enemies will fight and other matters beyond a leader's control. Nevertheless, there are certain factors that, when neglected, will undermine military reengineering. I believe these factors include

- exploiting technology systematically
- anticipating strategic demands
- securing sufficient political resources
- balancing the necessary military cultures
- improving performance through feedback and correction.

Perhaps the most sobering lesson from this historical review concerns the nonlinear nature of military reengineering. A transformation effort may achieve considerable success in attaining all but one of the necessary conditions, yet still fail badly.

Let us now discuss each of these factors in turn.

Exploiting Technology Systematically

Given the rapid pace of technological change in the 20th century, the willingness to exploit technological opportunities to their fullest potential is a prerequisite for significant process transformations.[3]

Few senior military commanders of the interwar era surpassed Guderian in his ability to transcend the 19th-century military hostility toward commercial machinery. He was widely known for his interest in even the most mundane technical aspects of military mechanization. Engineers and technicians would marvel at his clear-sighted questions when inspecting new procurement proposals.[4]

Seeking knowledge. The systematic pursuit of new technological opportunities means investing in new knowledge not traditionally associated with the military. The Reichswehr often sent elite officers to obtain Ph.Ds in engineering. The U.S. Army had their engineering officers do graduate work and set up the Army Industrial College. However formi-

---

[3] Military reengineering does not necessarily depend on technological innovation, of course. Napoléon Bonaparte was notorious for his conservative attitudes towards technological hardware. He eliminated France's balloon corps, discontinued the use of interchangeable parts in musket manufacturing, refused to employ the rifle, and dismissed Fulton's submarine-warfare proposals. On the other hand, he displayed a highly enlightened attitude toward military reengineering along scientific lines, as demonstrated by his reforms of the École Polytechnique and École du Metz (the advanced artillery and engineering academy), and by his generous funding of fundamental research in the physical and mathematical sciences.

[4] Charles de Gaulle, by contrast, was overwhelmed by the scores of unfamiliar technical subjects he had to confront when finally given a senior tank command in the late 1930s.

dable the Reichswehr was with its technical studies, it never matched the Americans with respect to detailed and comprehensive logistical studies. On the other hand, the basic R&D efforts of the U.S. Ordnance Department were paltry compared to its Soviet or Japanese counterparts. Tukhachevsky's Gas Dynamics Laboratory and the advanced R&D facilities associated with the Japanese navy evince this. The U.S. Army Air Corps relied extensively on NACA, much as the Luftwaffe depended on the outstanding aeronautical research center established under Goering's direct patronage. The contrast with innovative Italian and British officers is unmistakable: the relevance of their R&D products was routinely dismissed. The ultimate example was the intransigence that Whittle experienced when he tried to sell the RAF on his jet-propulsion ideas.

Exploiting uncertainty. Successful military reengineering campaigns must exploit, not simply tolerate, a state of research uncertainty and technological insecurity. The most dramatic military successes of the 20th century are closely associated with the ability to subject enemy forces to unanticipated processes. There is a direct relationship between the uncertainty of a process's success and the surprise of enemy forces. On the other hand, the greater the uncertainty is, the greater the risk of failure. Effective military reengineering essentially involves maintaining the delicate balance between the two.

The American and French armies were very cautious about armored warfare and began to reengineer only after the Germans demonstrated its utility in Poland. Such caution negated one kind of risk but led to failure on the battlefield. The Germans' tolerance of process risk essentially gave them a head start on the learning curve of tank warfare, which they maintained over the Anglo-Americans for virtually the entire war. The Russian tank forces likewise achieved a similar advantage over the Germans. While they never furnished a tank that performed as well as the Tiger I, they managed to apply sufficient upgrades to their T-34 and introduced the heavy IS-2 Joseph Stalin tank to neutralize that advantage.

The pursuit of technological risk comes at a price, however. Many seemingly excellent projects do ultimately fail. The German investment in strategic missile development at the expense of the turbo-jet fighter is a prime example. The rule of thumb appears to be that a nation should invest in rigorous training and educational processes that push the conceptual envelope, while also building a scientific and engineering knowledge base to minimize risks.

Anticipating Strategic Demands

The most challenging task in military reengineering often lies in orienting the process towards future strategic needs. Highly coordinated reengineering efforts accomplish little if the assumptions about how future wars will be fought prove fallacious. The French planned to fight precisely the war that the Germans strenuously sought to avoid. And the Germans delivered a war that the French had long considered impossible to wage without ruinous national human costs.

The Germans made their own mistakes, however, on another front. By December 1941, they found themselves fighting precisely the war against Russia that the Blitzkrieg tactics and logistics were not designed to sustain.

The U.S. Cavalry's "homeland security" focus on guarding the lengthy southwest border with Mexico up until the outbreak of World War II is another example of faulty strategic anticipations: a replay of World War I was not supposed to happen.

Such fallacious anticipations are especially dangerous for reengineering ambitions when a military organization believes its existing resources and capabilities are more than sufficient for any conceivable threat. Vivid examples include the Japanese navy's choice to disregard the threat of Allied submarines to its supply lines, and the unwillingness of the U.S. Army Air Corps and Luftwaffe to entertain the danger of radar-controlled interceptors to strategic bombers. Through the late 1930s, the French army's arrogant confidence in its ability to destroy a German offensive contrasts sharply with the Reichswehr's eternal terror at the prospect of facing multiple offensive actions.

On the positive side, military organizations have rarely surpassed the U.S. Marines and the Soviet Red Army with respect to strategic anticipation. The Marines based their amphibious warfare reengineering program on perhaps the most accurate strategic forecast of the century: Ellis's *Advanced Base Operations*. Few senior military commanders had Tukhachevsky's comprehensive grasp of the broad strategic demands that a Western invasion would place on the Soviet Union. Finally, few in Washington, D.C., anticipated more thoroughly the demands for industrial mobilization in World War II than the Army Industrial College during the 1930s. Such work went a long ways in offsetting the Army's weak anticipation of combat demands.

Securing Sufficient Political Resources

Resources are essential for any military reengineering effort, but they involve much more than increased financial budgets (and large budgets are not even necessary to lay the groundwork for reengineering). They involve both external support from civilian authorities and internal cooperation among the military hierarchy and military-industrial complexes. Such reengineering requires tangible as well as tactical assets. The U.S. Marine Corps received little financial support for its successful reengineering efforts—at least on a conceptual level—yet they enjoyed very encouraging relations with Franklin Roosevelt, who considered himself an "honorary Marine."[5] In spite of the financial and material support the Red Army received from Stalin, it was all but crippled by his purge of the senior officer corps in the late 1930s, which targeted the most strategically sophisticated and technically talented, starting with Tukhachevsky. The close support and large budgets the German and Italian armies enjoyed under their fascist rulers are clear enough. But the Italian army paid a stiff price for supporting Mussolini's dictatorship by having to expend scarce technical and material resources on the Ethiopian and Spanish campaigns. The Wehrmacht, likewise, received lucrative funding from Hitler, and was given considerable freedom to spend it on expansion during the 1930s. That benefit, however, came at the ultimately fatal price of abdicating its influence on broader strategic policies. The invasion of the Soviet Union was not exactly an enterprise proposed by the General Staff.

---

[5] For example, when Higgins first proposed his Eureka boat to the Marines in 1936 for testing, during the height of the military cutbacks during the Great Depression, he was turned down because the Bureau of Construction and Repair simply lacked sufficient funds. See Kenneth J. Clifford, *Amphibious Warfare Development in Britannia and America from 1920–1940*, Laurens: Edgewood, 1983, p. 112.

Military reengineering success, then, is not a straightforward function of public funding. Armed forces can receive generous funding and yet persist with their traditional doctrines. Also, military organizations operating on shoestring budgets, such as the U.S. and British armies, can use funding as an excuse for maintaining the status quo. It has recently been argued that, even with more lucrative funding during the interwar years, the U.S. Army would still have avoided the dramatic reengineering associated with mechanization: more funding would have merely purchased an expanded version of the original force.[6] At the same time, the Reichswehr and the U.S. Marine Corps persisted in achieving astonishing capabilities while operating within paltry budgets.

Securing the political resources to accomplish effective reengineering campaigns does not start with external financing. Rather, it begins with visionary leadership offering concrete aspirations that seize the imagination of subordinates and redirects their identity, while also convincing, weakening, or isolating vested opposing interests. Such vision can then lead to political support.

When strong leadership becomes too dogmatic and punishes objective critiques, however, the results can be devastating. The French army under Gamelin confused securing internal political support for Methodical Battle with isolating dissenting voices, including de Gaulle's and Estienne's. The Italian army was intent on withholding promotions from any officer that was too enthusiastic about mechanization or heavy weaponry. The service chiefs of the U.S. Army's bureaucratic units, along with many of their British counterparts, were notorious for equating objective criticism of existing doctrines with disloyalty, if not insubordination. Nothing will stimulate the creativity of a military organization more than the encouragement of and reward for rigorous intellectual debate, and nothing will discourage it more effectively than its suppression in the name of order and discipline. Such open debate becomes especially productive when managed by

---

[6] David E. Johnson, "From Frontier Constabulary to Modern Army: The U.S. Army Between the World Wars," in H. R. Winton and D. R. Mets, eds., *The Challenge of Change: Military Institutions and New Realities, 1918–1942*, Lincoln: University of Nebraska Press, 2000, pp. 203–4.

a centralized, yet objective or disinterested, command structure. The relative centralization of Tukhachevsky's and Seeckt's power, along with that of the U.S. Marine commandant's, stands in sharp contrast with the feudalistic or decentralized structure of the U.S. and British armies, where vested interests could resist change effectively. Unfortunately, when such centralized leadership is lacking in intellectual or innovative qualities, as in France and Italy at the time, the results could be disastrous. Thus, neither centralization nor decentralization is the formula for success. Stubborn little details—such as talent, wisdom, and military culture—do matter.

Balancing the Necessary Military Cultures

Another key challenge in reengineering a military organization is the effective alignment of the two fundamental, yet often conflicting, identities within modern Western forces: the scientific analyst and the heroic warrior. Archimedes, who repulsed the amphibious assaults of the Romans at Syracuse with his defensive siege machinery, is the classic embodiment of the analyst. His reputation was based primarily on his scientific or intellectual methodologies and their objective application, rather than on any particular weapon system. Alexander the Great, with his invincible leadership at the head of his frontal assaults—literally covered in blood, if accounts can be believed—is the classic manifestation of the warrior. His reputation was based primarily on his charismatic leadership skills and experiential knowledge of operating a particular weapon system—whether it was his personal sword, lance and bow, or an infantry phalanx. Virtually all the famous military commanders associated with the "Military Revolution" of early modern Europe strove to embody both paragons, especially Maurice of Nassau, the Marquis de Spinola, Gustavus Adolphus, Raimondo Montecuccoli, Vauban, Peter the Great, and Charles XII. The domination of siege warfare in early modern military operations strongly encouraged such a linkage between mathematical engineering analysis and aggressive combat leadership. The traditional engineering and mathematical orientation of West Point, especially after Mahan's reforms in the mid-19th century, also reflected this early modern Archimedean ideal—Robert E. Lee of the Army Corps of Engineers being its most notable result. Napoléon Bonaparte himself was the ultimate triumph of the union between the analytical and warrior spirit: he gained his initial military fame at Toulon as a scientific artillery officer who could also lead a bayonet charge. Scharnhorst, the founder of the Prussian General Staff during the Napoleonic Wars, followed Bonaparte's example. He initially taught mathematics and gunnery theory at the small Hanoverian artillery academy, yet also fought ferociously during the War of the First Coalition. Even the Duke of Wellington, hardly a military intellectual, argued after the Napoleonic Wars that solid mathematical analysis was essential for effective military leadership.[7]

Those military reengineering challenges of the interwar era that were associated with mechanization can be interpreted well within the framework of the analyst and warrior cultures. The armed forces that maintained a reasonable synthesis of the two cultures invariably accomplished much. Those forces in which one side predominated over the other invariably suffered. The senior commanders of the Fascist Italian army, for example, were dominated by their warrior faction. Commanding men and mules, according to the heroic massed-infantry actions of World War I, captivated their imagination. Incorporating seemingly awkward and unfamiliar weapons systems, not to mention devising efficient logistical strategies to maintain grimy motor engines, was not their idea of a glorious military career. Yet the influential air-power theorist Douhet demonstrated that the Italian military society was hardly lacking in analytical minds capable of astonishing vision. Likewise, the traditional Piedmontese military culture associated with the House of Savoy had placed great emphasis on training analytical engineering and artillery officers to defend their Alpine passes from French aggression since the 16th century. Lagrange, after all, was teaching analytical calculus at the School of Artillery and Military Engineering in Turin long before any other European military school attained such scientific sophistication. This tradition, however, was displaced by

---

[7] For a detailed analysis of the emergence of this analytical military culture during the early modern era, see: Steele and Dorland (2005).

a romantic warrior culture that could not stomach military processes extending beyond what World War I had established.

After the Great War, the French army was dominated by officers obsessed with reducing modern warfare to an analytical, systematic, and predictable affair dominated by artillery. Its officers effectively sought to destroy mobile field armies by employing the spirit of Vauban's classic siege tactics against unrelieved fortresses. This shift reflected the enormous casualties they suffered in the trench warfare of the Western front, where they persisted in conducting warrior-like infantry assaults with almost suicidal bravery. As their pre-1914 doctrine advocated, the human spirit will always overcome mere machinery, when advanced with sufficient determination. Perhaps the French reengineering along the lines of Methodical Battle reflected the trench-warfare annihilation of their warrior culture, especially in the infantry, leaving the more analytical and technical officers in control. The slaughter of the Western Front, on the other hand, did little to alter the traditional warrior mentality of the British line regiments, where the vast majority of their officer corps maintained an astonishing pride in their unwillingness to engage in serious analytical studies. In spite of the progress of the British tank experiments and debates, their impact on the regular cavalry, infantry, and even artillery officers was negligible.

The U.S. Marine Corps reveled throughout the 20th century in its much-publicized warrior culture. The Marines' success in reengineering to conduct offensive amphibious assaults against the central Pacific islands, however, rested on developing a sophisticated analytical culture as well. This is spelled out by the doctrinal studies of Major Ellis, along with the persistent FLEX maneuvers and the analyses and corrections that followed. Unlike the British marines, who failed to detach themselves from their traditional security and special-detachment duties, the U.S. Marine Corps willingly abandoned its traditional reputation as an auxiliary naval force.

The development of the U.S. Navy was remarkably different. The dreadnought revolution saw the rise of such analytical officers as Sims, especially with respect to gunnery and radio communications. Nevertheless, the battleship quickly generated a new warrior culture that focused, and even obsessed, on decisive fleet engagements. The effects of the U-boat in World War I did not change that view. Fortunately, the U.S. Navy's "corporate" attachment to the battleship did not preclude development of naval aviation and carrier warfare, in addition to the reinforcement of submarine warfare. Individual American naval officers displayed high degrees of analytical skill and imagination, as Moffett exemplified. They did not, however, attempt to engage in a fundamental reengineering away from the battleship and toward the aircraft carrier until Pearl Harbor left the Navy with little choice.

The genius of Seeckt in reengineering the Reichswehr was founded on his ability to synthesize the analytical ideals of the German General Staff and the tough combat traditions of the German soldier. While he replaced most of the Reichswehr's line officers of the Western Front with the educated analysts of the German General Staff, he also threw out any officer who failed to meet his exacting combat-leadership standards. In turn, Seeckt ensured that new junior officers completed a grueling four-year program, where they worked up through the enlisted ranks before being commissioned, to ensure such combat proficiency. The numerous artillery officers who served as generals in the Wehrmacht during World War II reveal the equally demanding analytical standards in the Reichswehr. Rommel was a typical line officer in World War I, with his warrior-like ambition for winning the coveted Pour le Mérite medal. Nevertheless, he engaged in an analytical study of infantry tactics after the war—perhaps related to his enthusiastic study of mathematics and his talent for *Kopfrechnung* (mental calculations). This culminated in his acclaimed book on infantry operations, which he published before assuming command of a panzer division. Similarly, Guderian's ability to synthesize a warrior's thirst for aggressive military action and an analyst's scientific objectivity and infatuation with high technology is easier revealed by his early military career. Initially commissioned in a light-infantry unit (which stressed mobility, of course), his first combat duties in World War I were in radio communications, followed by a General Staff education and motorized logistics command after the war.

No discussion of the need for balance, or synthesis, of the analytical and warrior cultures in modern military organizations would be complete without addressing General George Patton. He spared no effort in blustering about loving war, carrying an ivory-handled revolver into battle, proudly wearing an infantryman's helmet, and displaying other such modern-warrior gestures. He even speculated about a possible past life as Hannibal. Nevertheless, his analytical side was shown to be equally strong, with his pioneering command of an American tank brigade in World War I, his surprisingly insightful articles defending horse-cavalry troops during the 1930s, and his rigorous training program for armored desert warfare in 1942.

Improving Performance Through Feedback and Correction

Another condition for successful reengineering involves the establishment of corrective feedback mechanisms. This involves both the measurement of the organization's performance, expectations as to what constitutes success, the ability to ascertain the difference, and, finally, the means to institute the necessary changes. The newly modified force is then resubmitted to tests. Such actions reflect the virtual impossibility of successfully conceiving a major military process change based solely on rational study or intuitive understanding. For example, the Reichswehr's annual maneuvers and the Marine Corps' FLEX exercises usually revealed numerous problems when they tested new processes. These exercises proved to be paragons of military reengineering, however, because they were followed up with rigorous analyses of the results and rapid corrective action to eliminate any identified shortcomings. The British Army, in contrast, proved to be a first-rate force when conducting fundamental experiments of armored divisions during the late 1920s and early 1930s, but its failure to incorporate these lessons substantially into the active military units cost it dearly in France and North Africa during the early 1940s. The other extreme was the Red Army after Stalinist purges. Based on the single example of the marginal tank engagements of the Spanish Civil War, Stalin rejected years of armored-warfare studies and testing, culminating with Tukhachevsky's Deep Battle doctrine, on the eve of World War II. This case is of interest because it illustrates the dangers of overinterpreting results of individual exercises or battles.

It is indicative of the institutional effectiveness of the Wehrmacht during World War II that it was able to make a relatively smooth institutional shift from an offensive strategy of annihilation to a defensive strategy of attrition. That the effort failed partly because of the Nazi resistance to transforming the economy does not detract from this achievement. The transformation effort was manifested in particular by the heavy battle tanks the Germans introduced in the middle of the war, a process the British and American forces were effectively unable to match. These Allied forces essentially failed to modify the basic military doctrines developed before the war: the British with their uncoordinated regimental divisions of infantry, artillery, cavalry, and ultimately armor, and the Americans with their focus on high degrees of mobility and logistical efficiency at the expense of heavy firepower and armor. The Red Army, by contrast, made ruthless observations and corrections to achieve logistical support for its lengthy offensive actions into Eastern Europe, while also fielding heavy tanks, self-propelled artillery and rockets, and antitank guns in ever-increasing numbers. The thousands of military trucks and vehicles they received from the United States—material the Germans sorely lacked—mitigated the resulting stress.

No successful military reengineering effort is a finite affair with a distinct beginning, middle, and end. It invariably requires fine-tuning after its first tests in actual combat or experimental simulation. Again, the Wehrmacht's and Marine Corps' rigorous analyses and corrections after their initial baptisms in Poland and Tarawa reveal much about the strength of their reengineering methodologies. The Germans, in fact, were appalled at both the relatively poor performance of their own infantry forces and the failure of the panzer divisions to contribute decisively to the *Kesselschlacht,* or traditional encirclement campaign, against the Polish army. As a consequence, the senior leaders of the Wehrmacht convinced Hitler to postpone the invasion of France from the fall of 1939 until the spring of 1940 in order to "reengineer" their corrective training program.

References

Alexander, Martin, *The Republic in Danger: General Maurice Gamelin and the Politics of French Defence, 1933–1940,* Cambridge, Mass.: Cambridge University Press, 1992.

Bacevich, A. J., *The Pentomic Era: The U.S. Army Between Korea and Vietnam,* Washington, D.C.: National Defense University Press, 1986.

Bond, Brian, *British Military Policy Between the Two World Wars,* Oxford: Clarendon Press, 1980.

Boot, Max, *The Savage Wars of Peace: Small Wars and the Rise of American Power,* New York: Basic Books, 2002.

Bracken, Paul, *Reengineering and Information Technology: Relationships and Lessons Learned,* Santa Monica, Calif.: RAND Corporation, unpublished manuscript.

Bragadin, Marc Antonio, *The Italian Navy in World War II,* Annapolis, Md.: United States Naval Institute, 1957.

Campbell, John P., "Marines, Aviators and the Battleship Mentality, 1923–33," in Merrill L. Bartlett, ed., *Assault from the Sea: Essays on the History of Amphibious Warfare,* Annapolis, Md.: Naval Institute Press, 1983.

Clifford, Kenneth J., *Amphibious Warfare Development in Britannia and America from 1920–1940,* Laurens, N.Y.: Edgewood, 1983.

Corum, James S., *The Roots of Blitzkrieg: Hans von Seeckt and the German Military Reform,* Lawrence: University of Kansas Press, 1992.

———, "A Comprehensive Approach to Change," in Harold Winton and David Mets, eds., *The Challenge of Change: Military Institutions and New Realities, 1918–1941,* Lincoln and London: University of Nebraska Press, 2000.

Daley, John, "Patton Versus the 'Motor Maniacs': An Interwar Defense of Horse Cavalry," *Armor,* Vol. 106, No. 2, 1997, p. 13.

Davis, Paul K., *Planning Force Transformations: Learning from Both Successes and Failures,* Santa Monica, Calif.: RAND Corporation, unpublished, 2001.

Deighton, Len, *Blitzkrieg: From the Rise of Hitler to the Fall of Dunkirk,* New York: Alfred A. Knopf, 1979.

Deist, Wilhelm, "The Road to Ideological War: Germany, 1918–1945," in W. Murray, M. Knox, and A. Bernstein, eds., *The Making of Strategy: Rulers, States, and War,* Cambridge, Mass.: Cambridge University Press, 1994.

Delbruck, Hans, *History of the Art of War,* Lincoln, Nebr.: University of Nebraska Press, 1990.

Doughty, Robert Allan, "Firepower and the Methodical Battle," in *The Seeds of Disaster: The Development of French Army Doctrine, 1919–1939,* Hamden, Conn.: Archon, 1985, pp. 91–111.

———, "The French Armed Forces," in Allan Millet and Williamson Murray, eds., *Military Effectiveness,* Vol. II: *The Interwar Era,* Boston: Allen and Unwin, 1988.

Erickson, John, *The Soviet High Command: A Military-Political History,* Boulder, Colo.: Westview Press, 1984.

Guderian, Heinz, *Panzer Leader,* New York: Ballantine Books, 1957.

Hall, Bert S., *Weapons and Warfare in Renaissance Europe: Gunpowder, Technology, and Tactics,* Baltimore and London: Johns Hopkins University Press, 1997.

Hallahan, William H., *Misfire: The Story of How America's Small Arms Have Failed Our Military,* New York: Charles Scribner's Sons, 1994.

Hammer, Michael, and James Champy, *Reengineering the Corporation: A Manifesto for Business Revolution,* New York: Harper Business, 1993.

Heinl, Robert Debs, Jr., *Soldiers of the Sea: The United States Marine Corps, 1775–1962,* Annapolis, Md.: U.S. Naval Institute, 1962.

———, "The U.S. Marine Corps: Author of Modern Amphibious Warfare," in Merrill L. Bartlett, ed., *Assault from the Sea: Essays on the History of Amphibious Warfare,* Annapolis, Md.: Naval Institute Press, 1983.

Hofmann, George F., "Combatant Arms vs. Combined Arms: The U.S. Army's Quest for Deep Offensive Operations and an Operational Level of Warfare," *Armor,* Vol. 106, No. 1, 1997, pp. 9–10.

Horikoshi, Jiro, *Eagles of Mitsubishi: The Story of the Zero Fighter,* Seattle: University of Washington Press, 1981.

Hundley, Richard O., *Past Revolutions, Future Transformations: What Can the History of Revolutions in Military Affairs Tell Us About Transforming the U.S. Military?* Santa Monica, Calif.: RAND Corporation, MR-1029, 1999.

Johnson, David E., *Fast Tanks and Heavy Bombers: Innovation in the U.S. Army, 1917–1945,* Ithaca, N.Y.: Cornell University Press, 1998.

———, "From Frontier Constabulary to Modern Army: The U.S. Army Between the World Wars," in H. R. Winton and D. R. Mets, eds., *The Challenge of Change: Military Institutions and New Realities, 1918–1942,* Lincoln: University of Nebraska Press, 2000.

Kipp, Jacob W., "Military Reform and the Red Army, 1918–1941," in Harold R. Winton and David R. Mets, eds., *The Challenge of Change: Military Institutions and New Realities, 1918–1941,* Lincoln: University of Nebraska Press, 2000.

Knox, MacGregor, *Mussolini Unleashed 1939–1941: Politics and Strategy in Fascist Italy's Last War,* Cambridge, Mass.: Cambridge University Press, 1982.

———, *Hitler's Italian Allies: Royal Armed Forces, Fascist Regime, and the War of 1940–1943,* Cambridge, Mass.: Cambridge University Press, 2000.

Krepenevich, Andrew, "Cavalry to Computer: The Pattern of Military Revolution," *National Interest,* fall 1994, pp. 30–42.

Kroener, Bernard R., "Squaring the Circle: Blitzkrieg Strategy and Manpower Shortage, 1939–1942," in Wilhelm Deist, ed., *The German Military in the Age of Total War,* Dover, England: Berg Publishers, 1985.

Mallet, Robert, *The Italian Navy and Fascist Expansionism 1935–1940,* London: Frank Cass, 1998.

Marshall, Andrew W., "Some Thoughts on Military Revolutions," (Office of Net Assessment [OSD/NA] memorandum, Washington, D.C., July 27, 1993).

McFarland, Stephen L., *America's Pursuit of Precision Bombing, 1910–1945,* Washington, D.C.: Smithsonian Institution Press, 1995.

McNaugher, Thomas L., *New Weapons Old Politics: America's Military Procurement Muddle,* Washington, D.C.: Brookings Institution, 1989.

Messenger, Charles, *The Blitzkrieg Story,* New York: Charles Scribner's Sons, 1976.

Millett, Allan, and Williamson Murray, eds., *Military Effectiveness,* Vol. II: *The Interwar Years,* Boston: Allen & Unwin, 1988.

Millett, Allan R., "Assault from the Sea: The Development of Amphibious Warfare Between the Wars. The American, British, and Japanese Experiences," in William Murray and Allan Millet, eds., *Military Innovation in the Interwar Period,* Cambridge, Mass.: Cambridge University Press, 1996.

Mosier, John, *The Myth of the Great War: A New Military History of World War I,* New York: Harper Collins, 2001.

Murray, William, and Allan Millet, eds., *Military Innovation in the Interwar Period,* Cambridge, Mass.: Cambridge University Press, 1996.

Naveh, Shimon, *In Pursuit of Military Excellence: The Evolution of Operational Theory,* London: Frank Cass, 1997.

Nicolle, David, *The Janissaries,* Oxford: Osprey Publishing, 1995.

North, Douglas C., *Institutions, Institutional Change and Economic Performance,* Cambridge, Mass.: Cambridge University Press, 1990.

O'Connell, Robert L., *Sacred Vessels: The Cult of the Battleship and the Rise of the U.S. Navy,* Boulder, Colo.: Westview Press, 1991.

Odom, William O., *After the Trenches: The Transformation of U.S. Army Doctrine, 1918–1939,* College Station: Texas A&M University Press, 1999.

Parker, Geoffrey, *The Military Revolution: Military Innovation and the Rise of the West, 1500–1800,* Cambridge, Mass.: Cambridge University Press, 1988.

Perret, Geoffrey, *There's a War to Be Won: The U.S. Army in World War II,* New York: Random House, 1991.

Place, Timothy Harrison, *Military Training in the British Army, 1940–1944: From Dunkirk to D-Day,* London: Frank Cass, 2000.

Reber, John J., "Pete Ellis: Amphibious Warfare Prophet," in Merrill L. Bartlett, ed., *Assault from the Sea: Essays on the History of Amphibious Warfare,* Annapolis, Md.: Naval Institute Press, 1983.

Rice, Condoleezza, "The Making of Soviet Strategy," in Peter Paret, ed., *Makers of Modern Strategy from Machiavelli to the Nuclear Age,* Princeton, N.J.: Princeton University Press, 1986.

Rosen, Stephen Peter, *Winning the Next War: Innovation and the Modern Military*, Ithaca, N.Y.: Cornell University Press, 1991.

Sapolsky, Harvey M., *The Polaris System Development: Bureaucratic and Programmatic Success in Government*, Cambridge, Mass.: Harvard University Press, 1972.

Showalter, Dennis E., *Railroads and Rifles: Soldiers, Technology, and the Unification of Germany*, Hamden, Conn.: Archon, 1975.

Simpkin, Richard, *Deep Battle: The Brainchild of Marshal Tuckachevskii*, London: Brassey's Defence Publishers, 1987.

Smith, Denis Mack, *Mussolini's Roman Empire*, New York: Viking Press, 1976.

Smith, Holland M., and Percy Finch, *Coral and Brass*, Washington, D.C.: Zenger Publishing, 1979.

Steele, Brett D., "An Economic Theory of Technological Products," *Technological Forecasting and Social Change*, Vol. 48, No. 3, March 1995, pp. 221–224.

Steele, Brett D., and Tamera Dorland, eds., *The Heirs of Archimedes: Science and the Art of War Through the Age of Enlightenment*, Cambridge, Mass: MIT Press, 2005.

Stoecker, Sally W., *Forging Stalin's Army: Marshal Tukhachevsky and the Politics of Military Innovation*, Boulder, Colo.: Westview Press, 1998.

Strahan, Jerry E., *Andrew Jackson Higgins and the Boats That Won World War II*, Baton Rouge: Louisiana State University Press, 1994.

Trythall, Anthony John, *"Boney" Fuller: Soldier, Strategist, and Writer*, New Brunswick, N.J.: Rutgers University Press, 1977.

von Bertalanffy, Ludwig, *General Systems Theory: Foundations, Development, Applications*, New York: Braziller, 1968.

Weller, Donald M., "The Development of Naval Gunfire Support in World War II," in Merrill L. Bartlett, *Assault from the Sea: Essays on the History of Amphibious Warfare*, Annapolis, Md.: Naval Institute Press, 1983.

White, Charles, *The Enlightened Soldier: Scharnhorst and the Militärische Gesellschaft in Berlin, 1801–1805*, New York: Praeger, 1989.

Winton, Harold R., *To Change an Army: General Sir John Burnett-Stuart and British Armored Doctrine, 1927–1938*, Lawrence: University of Kansas Press, 1988.